There's Got to Be Something More

21 Days to Create a More Abundant, Purposeful, and Joyful Life

Kat Wells

Capucia LLC
211 Pauline Drive #513
York, PA 17402
www.capuciapublishing.com
Send questions to: support@capuciapublishing.com

Paperback ISBN: 978-1-954920-70-5
eBook ISBN: 978-1-954920-71-2
Library of Congress Control Number: 2023909198

Cover Design: Ranilo Cabo
Layout: Ranilo Cabo
Editor and Proofreader: Jennifer Crosswhite
Book Midwife: Karen Everitt

Printed in the United States of America

 Capucia LLC is proud to be a part of the Tree Neutral® program. Tree Neutral offsets the number of trees consumed in the production and printing of this book by taking proactive steps such as planting trees in direct proportion to the number of trees used to print books. To learn more about Tree Neutral, please visit treeneutral.com.

This book is dedicated to YOU, my reader.

May you always be searching for something more:

more things to create,

more people to love,

more laughter to share.

May you wake up to the truth of your magnificence and power,

knowing that you are exactly who the world

most needs you to be.

Contents

Foreword

The story that Kat Wells unfolds in *There's Got to Be Something More* is much more than a tale of the lessons she learned while transforming her life from one marked by hardship and discouragement to one of contribution, fulfillment, and abundance. What you'll find on these pages is a practical distillation of the powerful universal principles she discovered along the way and a precise formula you can begin applying immediately to release non-serving beliefs, reconnect with who you are at your essence, and become a more joyful and deliberate creator of your own life experience.

Like many people, myself included, Kat felt confused by and at the mercy of the contrasting experiences that manifested around her—including abuse, divorce, and estrangement from the vision she'd created for her life—until she began to recognize these turning points for what they were: irrefutable messages from the Universe urging her toward a more authentic self-expression than she previously thought possible. In this book, she walks you through the insights she gained at each step along her journey of becoming, offering powerful questions and practices at the end of each chapter to support you in making these actionable in your own life.

In the four years I've known Kat, she has demonstrated both a ravenous hunger for spiritual mastery and an ability to integrate the wisdom she has already attained. Having completed every course offered through the Quantum Success Learning Academy, which I founded in 2008, she is one of my most advanced and committed students. But beyond being a great teacher, Kat is genuinely a lovely person, and her down-to-earth personality comes through on every page. This generous work affords readers a very personal glimpse into the challenges and victories most of us will encounter along the way to realizing ourselves as the unbounded deliberate creators that each of us was born to be.

Christy Whitman
New York Times bestselling author
Scottsdale, Arizona

Preface

You may be wondering why I've chosen to create a new edition of *There's Got to Be Something More*. Since 2020, everyone's life has been turned upside down. I just happened to get a two-year head start.

On August 25, 2017, I was celebrating my twenty-seventh wedding anniversary with friends in Florida at a beach-side hotel and spa on a bright, sunny day. We were sitting by the pool when I received the news from my publisher that I had realized a life-long dream of becoming a number one best-selling author. The first edition of *There's Got to Be Something More* hit number one in three categories. I was beyond excited!

I had book signings and promotions scheduled for when we returned from vacation, and I was already enrolling clients in a new coaching program scheduled to begin in October.

But on October 13, my whole life was turned upside-down. My husband received the devastating news that his lungs were failing and he needed a double-lung transplant to survive.

The four months that followed were the most challenging months of my life. I was at the hospital daily, meeting with his team of doctors and holding out hope they would find a donor match. Mark was in pain. His life was slowly draining away, and there was nothing I could do except keep hoping for a miracle.

Then, on February 15, 2018, a few days before his birthday, we received the news a donor match had been found. The doctors and staff rushed into action. But just as I was leaving the pre-op holding area, the surgeon walked into the room to tell us the lungs had been compromised. They wouldn't be able to do the surgery. After four long months of preparing and waiting, all hope vanished. Mark passed away two days later.

Over the previous three years, I had mourned the loss of my mother, my young brother-in-law, and three close friends. I thought I knew grief, knew what to expect, but when Mark passed away, I didn't know if I would survive it this time.

For two years, the fog of grief enveloped me. I took my time and traveled slowly to keep my footing as best I could. I continued to study and take courses in psychology, physiology, brain science, bioenergetics, spirituality, and grieving. And, in 2019, I decided I was ready to begin again, to start over. So, I signed up for a Caribbean cruise scheduled for March 2020.

Yep! Just when I was ready to be part of the world again, I stepped off the cruise ship in Florida to a world shut down because of the pandemic. So, I chose to spend my time in "mandated seclusion" updating this book to serve a grieving world.

The tools and practices I have added at the end of each chapter of this new edition are those I used to navigate through my darkest days. Today, five years after Mark's passing, my life is more beautiful than I could have imagined. I have experienced more happiness, success, connection, excitement, and love than ever before.

My wish for you after the challenges of the past two years is, no matter where you are in life or what your struggles may be, that this new edition of *There's Got to Be Something More* gives you the tools and practices you need to create a life more beautiful than the one you left behind.

Introduction

When we believe we need to change the unchangeable, control the uncontrollable, undo what's been done, we can never be happy.

~ Kat Wells

Have there been times in your life when, no matter how hard you tried or how much you accomplished, nothing was working out quite the way you expected and you just couldn't see how things would ever get better? Yet, deep down you knew there had to be something more. Something you were missing.

I feel your pain; been there, done that, got the T-shirt!

In this book, I share personal stories of how I went from experiencing abuse, bankruptcy, divorce, miscarriage, losing my job, my home, my health, and wanting to end my life to manifesting a marriage of twenty-eight years, financial freedom, traveling the world for eight years, vibrant health, and a career I love.

Did it happen overnight? Nope. In fact, my journey was a long one, taking over thirty years and tens of thousands of dollars' worth of therapy, self-help books, CDs, seminars, and courses.

And then, one day in 2003, I discovered a book, *The Law of Attraction*, by Esther and Jerry Hicks, that sent me on a new path of learning and utilizing the Universal Laws to transform my life. Within two short years my life had changed dramatically. Millions of dollars began to flow into my life, chronic health issues were healed, and broken relationships were mended.

It is now my joy to share with you how to begin living an abundant, prosperous, and joyful life. For you, it doesn't have to take decades or thousands of dollars. It requires only a desire, a decision, and a dedicated practice to shift your focus. You can do this!

Where your focus goes, energy flows. As I began focusing on what I wanted with a feeling of excitement, letting the Universe handle the details, I was then inspired to take action and allowed the Universe to deliver my desire without limiting how or when it would come.

It's really that simple and not always easy. We've all been influenced by the beliefs and fears of others without realizing it. And we've been unconsciously acting on those beliefs for most of our lives, living by default. The good news is you can start shifting those beliefs today.

Like anything in this physical life, new behaviors take practice. The more you practice, the easier and more automatic the behavior becomes as new neural pathways are created in your brain. Pretty soon, the new behavior becomes your new set point, and shift happens.

At the end of each chapter in this book, in a section called Something More, you will discover the real reason you do the things you do and why change seems so hard. The next section, Something for You, teaches you simple and fun activities to uncover and transform the limiting beliefs holding you back from living the life of your dreams.

You may be inspired to read one chapter a day for twenty-one days, or you may prefer to read one chapter a week. Your timeline is a personal choice. What matters most is that you begin to incorporate the activities into your life at a pace that feels good to you.

Once you begin putting these activities into practice, you will gain a new perspective and notice more and more how the Universe is supporting you. The Law of Attraction will respond to your new perspective and new expectations by bringing you more and more to appreciate.

Once the momentum gets going, you will look back in the not-so-distant future and realize, as I did, that creating the life of your dreams was so much easier than you could have ever imagined.

My dream for you is that by sharing my journey, you will be inspired to live your life on purpose, discover your own inner wisdom, and love your life as much as I love mine.

Download your FREE Companion Workbook here

OR

www.SomethingMoreBook.com

CHAPTER 1

Salt and Pepper

The problems of the world cannot possibly be solved by skeptics or cynics whose horizons are limited by the obvious realities. We need men who can dream of things that never were.
~ John F. Kennedy

I loved sitting with my best friend on the front stoop of the duplex our families shared on the Army base at Ft. Sam Houston, Texas. We were six years old and spent a lot of time together. In fact, we were together so much of the time that everyone called us "Salt and Pepper." We innocently thought it was because we were a matched pair, not realizing it was because I was white and she was Black.

My friend and I had a daily ritual after school. We'd run inside our respective homes, grab our Barbie dolls and paraphernalia, and meet on the front stoop to play. My friend would always bring along her briefcase, which was actually a huge purse her mom had given her. And each day she would take two suckers out of it—the type with the little twisted loop handles—a red one for me and a green one for her. As we ate our candy, we would use our Barbie dolls to reenact our day together in Miss Sweetland's first-grade class.

One autumn afternoon, it suddenly occurred to me that my friend's Barbie doll had white skin. Curious, I asked her, "Why don't you have a Black Barbie?"

She shrugged her little shoulders, looked at me, and said, "Mommy said they don't make Black ones."

"Why not?" I asked. "Mine has blond hair and blue eyes like me. Yours should look like you."

I told her we should make her Barbie Black, and then I ran inside my house and emerged a minute later with my box of crayons. I pulled out the black one and tried to color her Barbie's face, but the wax crayon wouldn't stick to Barbie's hard-rubber surface.

"Thanks for trying," she said. "I'll just keep pretending."

Later that week, on Friday, November 22, 1963, my friend and I were eating our sack lunches together at school when an announcement was made over the public-address system. President Kennedy had been shot. It was total chaos at the school; administrators were yelling, and teachers were crying as they herded all the students into the library. Sitting on the floor watching the news, my friend and I were linked arm in arm and crying because we didn't understand what was happening.

When the newsman announced that Kennedy had been taken to the hospital, the school released us, and my friend and I walked back to our duplex together, holding hands, with tears streaming down our faces.

When we arrived home, we could see that our mothers had been crying too. Our fathers were in the Army Central Intelligence Division and had already been summoned to Dallas. Acting as good military wives, our mothers tried to remain composed and keep us from worrying. They handed us our white Barbie dolls and sent us outside to play as if to say, "Nothing has changed."

We were transferred to another military base a few months later, and I never saw my little friend again.

The death of President Kennedy, the fearful reactions by those in authority, our mothers' tears, and what appeared to be the disappearance of my father into danger taught me to expect the world to be a scary and dangerous place.

Ironically, after I wrote this chapter, I was talking to my mother about this incident and asked her if she happened to remember my friend's name. She smiled and said, "Her name was Barbara, but everyone called her Barbie."

To my friend: I hope you no longer have to pretend to be something other than your beautiful self. We will always be connected.

಄ ಄ ಄

Something More

Have you ever felt disconnected, separate from the world and all the people around you? Have you felt like everyone else is on a journey to somewhere, but you're not invited? As babies, we believe we're the center of the Universe and that everyone is here for us. We feel connected to people, animals, and the earth. We are not yet tied to an identity of who we are. But society and life experience soon teach us separateness. We learn it through prejudices—racial, religious, and societal—that others hold and pass on to us. We learn it through judging others and ourselves, by stereotyping and pigeonholing the people we meet and even those we don't know.

This feeling of separateness comes from the ego, which is a fear-based, survival-centric identity developed before the age of five or six years old. It serves to protect you and to help you meet the challenges in life. Safety is its highest priority. That's why I prefer to call the ego the protective personality.

Your ego's beliefs about who you are, your value, and your worthiness are rooted in the events and experiences of your childhood. These experiences also determine whether you perceive the world as a safe or a dangerous place.

For example, the fear of abandonment I experienced the day of Kennedy's assassination was triggered by the disappearance of my father and the fearful reactions of the adults in my world. This fear of abandonment would become a pattern in my life I did not consciously choose. It was subconsciously chosen for me by my protective personality from a child's experience and perspective. Over time, other life events reinforced this fear.

It wasn't until I began to consciously observe and challenge my beliefs that I realized I had the power to change them. Identifying core beliefs is where the healing journey begins.

If you're ready for something more in your life, begin by exploring and perhaps challenging the beliefs you hold. How do you know what your beliefs are? By reflecting on the current condition of some aspect of your life that you would like to change and noticing how you feel. Perhaps it's disappointment, frustration, anger, or maybe even hopelessness. Your emotions are telling you that you have a core belief in opposition to your desire.

Next, ask yourself, "What would I need to believe about myself, others, or the world to create this circumstance?" For example, when I asked myself this question regarding an abusive marriage I didn't know how to escape, I realized I had a belief that to be loved, I had to please others and do things I didn't want to do so they wouldn't abandon me. This awareness gave me the courage to leave the marriage, live on my own, and eventually create a loving relationship that lasted thirty years.

෪෪෪

Something for You

Below, I offer a few questions to explore so you may begin reflecting on the beliefs you currently hold. Please remember, there is no judgment here, simply clarity. By identifying your beliefs, you become empowered to consciously keep those that serve you and release those that do not.

As you begin this journey to something more, I invite you to use a journal to record your answers to the questions at the end of each chapter and any insights you may have along the way. Writing is an opportunity to communicate with your subconscious and to create a benchmark of where you started.

- What beliefs do you hold about yourself?
- What beliefs do you hold about the world?
- What beliefs do you hold about others?
- Which of these beliefs continue to serve you and why?
- Which of these beliefs would you like to release or shift?

CHAPTER 2

Basic Training

Even the darkest moment has within it an element of love —
the need for it, the lack of it, or the desire to create more.

~ Sanaya Roman

Summer 1978

I'm in the hospital," he said in a mechanical, nonhuman voice. "Come get me."

"What's wrong?" I asked.

"Just come get me. Don't tell anybody," he said and hung up.

I jumped in the car and drove the sixty miles to the military base hospital in San Antonio. When I entered the waiting room, there were several recruits with shaved heads dressed in camouflage fatigues standing in a line against the far wall. They all looked identical.

Suddenly, one of the recruits ran toward me yelling, and the military police sprang into action. It took five policemen to tackle the man to the ground and subdue him. They handcuffed his hands behind his back and jerked him to his feet. It was my husband, Paul.

Wild-eyed and red-faced, he struggled against the handcuffs, and with one loud yell he broke loose from the grip of the police and lunged toward me again. The military police again grabbed him and shoved him against the wall.

In a quiet, childlike voice he said to me, "Please take me home."

Two huge orderlies dressed in white joined the military police and removed Paul from the waiting room. It was the last time I saw him for several weeks.

The doctors told me Paul had suffered a mental breakdown during his first week of basic training. He had not slept for five days and had lost control. They were going to admit him to the psychiatric ward and would call me when it was safe to visit.

Three weeks passed without a word from the hospital. Meanwhile, I kept my promise to Paul to tell no one he was in the hospital. As far as our families knew, he was still in basic training. But keeping his secret was beginning to take its toll on me.

I was losing weight, and I couldn't sleep, worrying about what was wrong with Paul and whether he would get better. Would I be responsible for taking care of him? Was it my fault? Would he hurt me? I desperately wanted to talk to someone, but I had made a promise to Paul that I wouldn't tell anyone.

When the hospital finally called to say he could have visitors, I was at first relieved and then terrified. I had never been in a psychiatric ward. Scenes from the movie *One Flew over the*

Cuckoo's Nest came to mind, and for the first time I realized how helpless and unprepared I was for what might lie ahead.

On the long drive to the military hospital, my thoughts wandered back to my childhood. While growing up in Army housing with a father who was a highly decorated war veteran and a raging alcoholic—a man fighting demons none of us could understand—I lived in constant fear.

Was this to be my life forever? I was only nineteen. When Paul and I married a year ago, I thought I'd finally found happiness, that I'd be safe and secure. And though we'd been yelling at each other a lot over the past few months and Paul shoved me against the wall a couple of times, I thought it was just his frustration at being fired from his job. But the rage that exploded from him at the hospital was about much more than that.

As I pulled into the hospital parking lot, I felt sick to my stomach. I wished I had someone to turn to, someone to help me through this. But there was no one.

Inside the hospital, I was asked to sign some papers, and an escort was assigned to accompany me to the psychiatric ward. As we rode the elevator in silence, fear overwhelmed me, and my knees buckled.

My escort grabbed my arm. "Are you okay?" he asked.

"I don't know what to expect. The doctors didn't tell me anything," I replied.

The elevator doors opened, and he led me to a chair beside the desk where a nurse had me sign more papers. She opened a security door, and my escort led me to a doctor's office. The walls were pale Army green. The hard tile floor and gray metal desk and black chairs added to the clinical, cold feeling.

The doctor introduced himself and said, "Before we start, I want you to know that this is not your fault. Paul's problems started long before he met you."

I thought, *What a weird thing to say. Why would his problems in basic training be my fault?*

"What's going on?" I asked. "No one's told me anything."

"He's had a severe breakdown. He doesn't know his own name; he can't function with his basic needs. He doesn't remember his family members or his friends. The only one he remembers is you," he said.

"He remembers me, but not his own name?" I asked in disbelief. "What happened during basic training? He was only here for a week."

"I can't share the details with you except to tell you he was on the verge of this breakdown before he joined the military. Basic training is designed for this purpose, to make sure recruits are physically and mentally ready for training and military service."

"I don't understand what's happening. Is he going to recover? What am I supposed to do?"

"He will be here a long time. At least a year. The best thing you can do for him is to come visit as often as you can. He's had extreme violent outbursts, so we have him on heavy sedation. You will not be alone with him at any time. The orderly can take you to his room if you'd like to see him. Do you want us to contact his family?"

Everything was moving too fast. I couldn't believe this was happening. Did I want to see him? Should I tell his parents or keep my promise? I wanted to run away from this nightmare.

"Do we have to tell his family?" I asked. "He wanted me to keep it a secret."

"Not today. But eventually they'll have to know. He's only nineteen, and he'll need support to recover once we release him. You can't do this on your own."

For better or for worse,

For richer, for poorer,

In sickness and in health,

Until death do us part...

Oh my God, what's going to happen to me, to my life?

"I'd like to see him," I said.

He motioned for an orderly. "Paul's in a private room, and he's restrained. When you're ready to leave, the orderly will escort you downstairs to the lobby. I'm sorry for what you must be going through—you're so young to be dealing with this."

If he only knew. I'd been dealing with this my entire life.

The orderly lead me through the recreation area, which looked like a large living room with game tables, sofas, chairs, and a large television. Young men and a few women were scattered around the room, some playing cards and others watching television. One man dressed in pajama bottoms, a white T-shirt, and hospital slippers was simply standing in the middle of the room staring into space, swaying back and forth from one foot to the other. Everyone in the room seemed to be moving in slow motion.

After we crossed the recreation room, we continued down a long corridor with closed doors on either side. The stark florescent lighting and the smell of antiseptic were foreboding.

When we reached Paul's room, I took a deep breath as the orderly led me inside. I wasn't prepared for the devastation I felt seeing my husband strapped to the hospital bed, restraints around his ankles and wrists, staring at me with empty eyes as if his life had been drained out of him.

I walked over to his bed, but he didn't seem to recognize me. I touched his hand, and he clasped it into a fist.

"It's best if you don't touch him," the orderly warned.

As I looked around the bare room, I noticed the few personal effects he had were lined up with precision on his dresser: his wallet, military identification card, hairbrush, toothbrush, wristwatch, wedding ring, and a photo of me.

"He doesn't like anyone touching his things," the orderly said. "In the mornings, he's usually calm enough to be out of his restraints. The first thing he does is to go over to his dresser and straighten his things. But he still hasn't remembered how to use his hairbrush or toothbrush. We have to remind him every morning."

I burst into tears.

The orderly led me out of the room and into the hallway. I leaned against the wall for support and slid to the floor, sobbing. The orderly sat across from me, trying to comfort me with words I could not understand. Any hopes for happiness, safety, or security had vanished.

"Ma'am, let's get you downstairs," he said as he stood and helped me to my feet.

As we walked back through the recreation room, I looked over at the man in pajamas, still swaying back and forth while looking out into space and understood his pain.

The next morning, I woke up thinking I had been having a nightmare. I didn't remember getting into my car or driving the sixty miles back home. None of it felt real until I found the doctor's business card in my purse.

I burst into tears again and realized I had to break my promise and tell Paul's parents. I couldn't handle this alone.

> *We promise according to our hopes and perform*
> *according to our fears.*
>
> ~ Anonymous

For over four months I traveled the 120-mile round trip every day to visit Paul for one hour. He was making progress. He was able to groom himself and dress himself and tie his own shoes. He was beginning to remember more details about his life and his family. He was getting his appetite back. The doctor was hopeful that he would be released much sooner than anticipated.

Although I had told his parents about his situation, they never visited him in the hospital. They wouldn't even allow me to talk to them about him or his condition. I was still handling this alone.

Around five months into his treatments, the doctor informed me Paul was ready to have a day pass. He suggested I take him out to lunch and then bring him back to the hospital.

I wasn't as confident as the doctor that it was a good idea. What if something set him off, and he lost control? There would be no one around to protect me. After all, he had mentioned several times in the beginning of his treatments that it was my fault he was in the hospital.

What if he still blamed me?

Was I safe?

But Paul seemed so excited and happy to have the chance to leave the hospital for a while that I conceded. He had been working hard, going to sessions with the doctors and to group sessions without resistance.

The doctor's diagnosis was bipolar disorder, a manic-depressive illness that causes severe shifts in mood, energy, and the ability to carry out day-to-day tasks. Along with psychotherapy, they were treating him with medication. He hadn't had an outburst in a while. They believed he was stable. In fact, they were hopeful he'd be released in a few weeks.

So, we headed out to have lunch at a nearby restaurant. They had given Paul a day pass and said we could stay out as long as we liked but to return by 4:00 p.m. Unfortunately, they said it in front of Paul who, once we exited the hospital, decided he wanted to go home.

"We can't go all the way home, Paul. That's sixty miles away. That means I would have to drive two hundred forty miles today."

"I don't care. I want to go home. Take me home," he demanded.

I was afraid to disagree with him for fear it would set him off. So I drove the sixty miles to the house. When we arrived, Paul wandered around looking at everything while I fixed something to eat. After lunch, I suggested we start driving back since we had just over an hour before his curfew.

He stared directly into my eyes and said, "I'm not going back."

Fear shot through my body. I started to panic.

"Paul, you have to go back," I said as calmly as I could. "You need a little more time to get well."

"I'm not going back!" he yelled.

"But Paul, you're still in the military. They'll come arrest you, and then you might have to stay in longer."

"NO!" he screamed as he shoved me against the wall.

I just froze, not knowing what to do, and then I felt as if I'd left my body. I don't know what happened. I don't know what was said. It was as if I went to sleep and when I awoke, I was in my car driving Paul back to the hospital.

He was agitated, his body was shaking, and he was rocking back and forth in his seat. I drove eighty-five miles per hour back to San Antonio, hoping to make it to the hospital before Paul lost control.

When we entered the psychiatric ward, he walked away without a word and never looked back.

"How did it go?" the doctor asked as he escorted me to his office.

"It went to hell the minute we stepped outside this hospital!" I yelled. "He's out of control. I can't believe you thought it was safe for me to be alone with him!"

"Bipolar disorder is unpredictable. Paul's moods can flip quickly and be triggered without warning. He's on medication, but finding the right combination and the best dosage isn't simple."

How had this happened? Was it possible that I had married into the same violent and unpredictable life that I was trying so hard to escape? Why didn't I see that he was unstable when I met him? How was I supposed to deal with this when the doctors don't even know what to do?

I felt totally alone and unprepared to handle any of this. There was no support from family or from the military. I simply moved through each day the best I could. I continued traveling 120 miles daily to visit Paul, hoping that if he knew I was there for him that the doctors could fix him, and somehow, we'd have a normal life.

Two months later, Paul was released from the hospital and discharged from the military. There was no follow-up, no support, no information offered to me about how to live with his diagnosis. His family still would not talk about it, and Paul refused to get any kind of help.

A month after his discharge, Paul stopped taking his medication, and the drastic mood swings returned. He kept getting fired from jobs because of his angry outbursts. He started drinking heavily, and that made everything even worse.

I was always on guard, never knowing what would set him off. Each time he hit me or shoved me, he'd see my reaction, and it was like a switch had been flipped. He'd immediately apologize and be upset with himself and beg me to forgive him, promising not to do it again. I knew he was sick, and I wanted to help him, but I was scared.

Life became an emotional rollercoaster. For the next two years, I rode the ups and downs of his illness with him, hoping God would answer my prayers for help.

When Paul applied for a construction job in Bay City where they were building a new power plant, he was excited about moving away from San Antonio, away from his family and the reminders of his past. He thought it would give him a fresh start. It was the first time in three years I'd seen him hopeful and enthusiastic.

When he heard he'd gotten the job, I thought my prayers had been answered. Like Paul, I believed if we just moved away and started over, things would get better. And they were, for a few months.

He worked nights, and I worked days as a volunteer for a local church. We didn't see a lot of each other, and as months went by, he seemed to be working longer and longer hours. Or so he said.

I started to notice a change in his behavior. He'd get angry with me and leave the house for days at a time. When he'd return, he'd tell me he stayed at work to get overtime and just slept in the bunkhouse on site.

He'd show me extra cash. I thought it strange that instead of bringing me his check to deposit, he'd started cashing it. All kinds of thoughts were going through my mind, but I was too afraid to challenge him.

A few weeks later, I was home alone in my bedroom and heard someone come in the front door. Paul was supposed to be at work, but it was his voice filling the hall as he looked for me.

"It's all your goddamn fault! None of this would be happening to me if I hadn't married you!" he screamed. Paul headed toward me with clenched fists.

"What do you mean? What are you talking about?" I asked, trying to keep my voice calm.

"I got fired again!" he yelled.

"What happened?" I asked, as I tried to think of where to run.

"They caught me dealing drugs and said if I didn't leave immediately they were going to call the police!"

He pushed me against the wall, and I lost control. All my fear and anger erupted into rage, and I shoved him back. He grabbed me by the throat; I couldn't breathe and passed out.

When I regained consciousness, Paul was gone.

I raced through the house gathering everything I could, threw it in my car, and headed for San Antonio, back to my parents' home, the only other place I had to go.

My parents did not support my decision to leave my husband and grudgingly allowed me to stay with them if I promised to work things out with Paul. But I knew I could never go back.

I got a job, and as soon as I had enough money, I hired an attorney and filed for divorce. There was a mandatory ninety-day waiting period before it would be final, and I lived in constant fear Paul would retaliate.

Before I got into my car, I'd look in the back seat. When I left the house or the office, I'd scan the area, worried he'd be waiting for me. When I went out late with friends, I made sure someone dropped me off at my parents' house.

After a couple of months had passed without any news from Paul, I began to relax. When I received notice that my divorce was final, my parents were in Nebraska visiting my uncle in the hospital. I was home alone and wanted to go out, so I called some friends from the office, and we all headed to a local country-western dancehall.

It was Friday night, and the place was packed. We danced, played pool, and at 2:00 a.m. went to an all-night diner to eat. Afterward, a friend dropped me off at my parents' house and waited until I was inside before driving off.

I went to the back door in the kitchen and let our German shepherd, Princess, inside. As she followed me toward my bedroom, there was a knock on the front door. I thought maybe my friends had returned, but when I opened the door Paul was standing there, wild-eyed, just like that day at the hospital.

He must have been watching the house and knew that my parents weren't home. As I tried to slam the door shut, he shoved me back. Princess bared her teeth and jumped for his throat. In a split second, he jerked the door to block her, and

Princess hit it full force with all her weight. I slammed my body into the door and slid the bolt. Princess kept barking and hitting the door with her body.

When she stopped barking and I heard his car tires burning rubber down the street, I slid to the floor and sobbed uncontrollably.

I would never feel safe again.

&CB&CB&CB

Something More

As children, we create stories from patterns we observe around us, which become our truth. I observed my mom's lonely struggle with my father's alcoholism and learned at a young age to keep secrets. As an adult, I subconsciously repeated those patterns.

Why did I stay in an abusive relationship for so long? I had a belief that it was normal because it was all I knew. I was doing the best I could, the best I knew how. My mother stayed married to my dad for thirty-five years, so I believed I should stick it out too. And my family pattern of keeping secrets kept me from seeking help. It wasn't until I feared for my life that I found the courage to leave.

Our beliefs are simply patterns of thought we keep thinking. These thoughts then influence the way we feel, which affects the choices we make and the actions we take. That's how thoughts become things. The good news is we have complete control over our thoughts. We can change them anytime. If you change your thoughts, you change your beliefs, and you change your life.

It sounds simple, but it takes courage and a willingness to take an honest look at what is and isn't working in our life. This isn't about judging your past or the choices others are making; it's about creating the life of YOUR dreams.

Remember, most of your beliefs about yourself and the world were created before you were six years old. And these patterns of thought have gathered more and more evidence over time, so they feel very real.

We think we base our beliefs on evidence. What if we simply arrange evidence to fit our beliefs?

For example, when I was a public school teacher, I also coached a UIL (University Interscholastic League) Impromptu speaking competition for fifth- and sixth-grade students. For impromptu speaking, the students draw three topics out of a bowl and choose one to prepare a speech on. They have only three minutes to prepare a speech, even if they know nothing or very little about the topic. It always amazed me what their creative minds could accomplish and how convincingly they presented their topics.

One day, during our bus ride to a district meet, one of my students was excitedly telling her teammates about her recent trip to Disney World. She shared all her fun activities and adventures. She gave great details about the rides, costumes, fireworks, food, and the new friends she made. She had everyone's attention, including mine.

Later that day during the competition, one topic she drew was: "My Terrible Experience at Disney World." I thought for sure she would have picked one of the other two topics, but she chose Disney World. Her story about the crowded bathrooms, the terribly long waiting lines for rides, the hot pavement, and how she lost her beloved Mickey Mouse ears was so convincing that she won first place.

She simply arranged her facts to support her topic, just like we arrange evidence to fit out beliefs. The difference is she consciously supported her story; our protective personality (ego) subconsciously supports ours.

❦ ❦ ❦

Something for You

If you're ready to discover what might be holding you back from living the life of your dreams, let's return to your journal and consider the following questions. Below, I have listed six key areas where beliefs impact our lives. I encourage you to work with the first one that pops into your awareness, the one that stands out.

It's not necessary to explore them all right now. Your core beliefs are like a woven tapestry, all the threads are interconnected. As you start to shift beliefs in one area of your life, all areas of your life will begin to improve.

- Which one of these key areas do you most want to shift?
  - Spiritual
  - Financial
  - Relationship
  - Career
  - Family
  - Health
- What belief patterns in this area would you most like to change? Journal about this in detail.
- What is the new belief you choose to hold? (Hint: It's usually the opposite of the current belief)

Challenge

Start looking for evidence to support this new belief. Keep track of the evidence in your journal.

CHAPTER 3

Message in the Mirror

The woods are lovely, dark and deep,
But I have promises to keep,
And miles to go before I sleep,
And miles to go before I sleep.

~ Robert Frost

Fall 1987

I felt dizzy, as if I might pass out. I clutched the bathroom sink trying to hold onto consciousness. The baby was almost imperceptible, floating in blood that seemed to fill the toilet bowl. Another miscarriage.

As I steadied myself and splashed cold water on my face, I heard the theme song from *Miami Vice* playing on the television in the living room where my second husband, Robert, sat in a recliner, oblivious.

Why was I being punished?

What had I done that was so bad that I deserved this on top of everything else?

Was it because I jumped into a second marriage with Robert only a few short months after my divorce from Paul?

I hadn't told my husband that I might be pregnant. I was afraid to.

Even though we'd been married eight years, our marriage and our lives were a mess. He was unemployed, our mobile home was being repossessed because we had filed for bankruptcy, and the company I worked for was going out of business.

As I stared at my pale, thin face in the mirror, an overwhelming feeling of a presence surrounded me. Then a vision appeared. It was a small girl, about two years old with golden curls and a sad face. She held her hands as if in prayer and stood awkwardly with braces on both of her legs.

A crippled child needs me? Was this a hallucination caused by the loss of blood?

I kept blinking my eyes, but she remained. It felt like we were having a conversation, as if she was asking me for help. Somehow, I felt relieved. As if there was a bigger purpose for what I was going through.

"What are you doing?" Robert asked, startling me.

"I'm feeling faint. I think I just had a miscarriage?"

Without saying a word, he walked over to the toilet, looked inside, then flushed it.

As he walked past me into the living room to watch television, I silently closed the bathroom door and curled up in the fetal position on the cold tile floor, rocking back and forth, sobbing for my baby and for me.

The following weeks passed in a hazy stupor. I felt as if I were a spectator watching my life pass before my eyes, but there was no emotion. Our mobile home was towed away, and the rectangular patch of dirt outlined in the grass was all that remained.

We found a cheap apartment while I still had a job, but the boxes stood stacked, unopened, against the living room wall. I didn't care anymore. I was simply going through the motions of daily existence.

Why was life so hard?

No matter what I did, nothing ever seemed to work out for me. I followed the rules, I did whatever I could to please others, but it didn't seem to matter. My second marriage was now hanging by a thread.

Day after day, Robert sat in his chair, surrounded by unopened boxes, watching reruns of *Miami Vice* while I went to work. He didn't seem interested in finding a job. I begged him to go for job interviews to receive his unemployment check.

We still had to pay child support for his daughter, even though his ex-wife had illegally taken her out of the state and disappeared with her boyfriend. We had attorney's fees and fees for the private investigator we'd hired to find them.

Feeling hopeless and depressed, I suggested marriage counseling, but Robert refused.

"You're the one with the problems," he yelled, "not me."

I didn't know what to do. I was desperate. I was losing everything, again. I went to the guest bedroom and climbed into bed. It was only seven o'clock, but I was exhausted.

The next few days were hectic at work as employees were finishing up business before the doors closed for good. I had sent out my resume to other businesses and had a couple of interviews scheduled for the following week.

My coworkers were excited for me, and it gave them hope, but I didn't care. I was numb from a grief that no one around me knew about. I didn't see the point in sharing my troubles with others who had their own worries. Besides, what could they do? Nothing ever worked out for me anyway.

I was surprised at my own self-pity, but I couldn't seem to shake it. I was spiraling downward, and there was nothing to grasp to stop the fall.

As I methodically cleared out my desk on our last day at work and placed my personal belongings into boxes, I thought of the boxes still unopened in my living room. Everything from my life was packed up as if to say goodbye.

It was dark outside, and a light rain was falling as I carried the last box from my office to my car. I was holding back tears, afraid that if I started crying I would never stop.

I put the car in gear, cranked up the radio to drown out my thoughts, and headed home in the rain. And then the theme song for *Miami Vice*, "In the Air Tonight" by Phil Collins, came on the radio, reminding me of all the pain waiting for me at home. As I drove down the dark, winding road surrounded by trees, the intensity of the song's beat put me in a trance, as if I were watching myself from outside my body. The lyrics expressed all my desperate and lonely feelings.

I realized in that moment that I just couldn't take it anymore. If this was life, I was done. I stepped on the gas, steering toward the trees.

A booming voice, so loud that it filled the car, came from nowhere: "WE'RE NOT DONE YET!"

Everything went black.

I don't know how long it was before I regained consciousness or what happened, but I awoke with my car in a ditch facing the road. I did not hit a tree. The car was still running, and I was safe. I burst into tears—tears of sadness and despair, tears of guilt and regret, tears of anger, and finally, tears of joy.

In that moment, I felt the presence of a great love and knew there was a purpose to my life. Now I understood the message in the mirror. That handicapped little girl was the injured child within me pleading to be healed.

A man's true wealth is the good he does in the world.
Beauty is eternity gazing at itself in the mirror. But you
are eternity, and you are the mirror.

~ Kahlil Gibran

ෆෆෆ

Something More

In my darkest hour, I surrendered, and a love beyond measure enveloped me, sparking a flicker of hope that illuminated my path and changed the course of my life forever.

In that moment, my Soulful Self, my Divine Self, felt integrated with the fabric of the Universe and connected to All That Is. For the first time in my life, I knew my worthiness and understood there was *something more* to this physical life than living in fear and pain and struggle. It was time to find my way back to love.

The source of love is the soul, the immortal part of you. Whenever you feel joy, love, appreciation, gratitude, passion, happiness, freedom, enthusiasm, you are in alignment with the soul.

The source of fear is the protective personality, the human part of you that developed before the age of six and was influenced by the people and events of your life. Whenever you feel worry, blame, anger, jealousy, guilt, unworthiness, powerlessness, fear, judgment, you are NOT in alignment with the soul. You are reacting to the perceptions of the ego.

Every experience you have in your life encourages the alignment of your protective personality with your soul. This alignment allows the personality to serve the soul, to serve love.

In his book, *The Seat of the Soul*, Gary Zukav states, "When the energy of the soul is recognized, acknowledged, and valued, it begins to infuse the life of the personality. When the personality comes fully to serve the energy of its soul, that is authentic empowerment."

Creating the *something more* I was searching for was not about blaming the ego or trying to override or ignore it. It was about reconnecting with my Soulful Self, my Divine Self. And that's what I want for you too. Authentic empowerment.

𝒞𝒞𝒞

Something for You

How do you begin to align your soul and personality to realize the *something more* you've been searching for? By looking in the mirror.

At the beginning of my journey back to love, I engaged the help of a brilliant psychiatrist, Sandy, to help me through the first two months. I knew I could not travel this journey alone. My life was evidence of that.

During our first session, Sandy gave me what I thought was a simple assignment. She asked me to look in the mirror, deeply into my own eyes, every morning for the next week and say, "I love you." What I didn't realize was how hard it would be.

The first day, before I could get the words out, I looked into my own eyes and just began to sob. I couldn't hold my own gaze. The second day was the same. By the end of the week, I could speak the words, but I couldn't maintain eye contact with myself. Honestly, I just said the words while looking at my reflection, all the while critiquing everything that was wrong with me in my mind.

Why was such a simple assignment so difficult? I had lived so long feeling unworthy that I couldn't connect with my soul, my Divine Self.

With Sandy's help, I eventually made the connection. And this time the tears were tears of joy. That was in 1988. To this day, whenever I notice I'm being overly critical of myself, I will stop, look in the mirror, and speak loving kindness. This is the soul infusing the life of the personality (ego) with love.

Your eyes are the windows to your soul. This mirror exercise will allow you a deeper connection to the truth of who you are. If you're ready, I invite you to do this exercise for at least a full week:

- Choose a beginning date.
- In private, look in the mirror, deeply into your eyes.
- Say, "I love you," with conviction, really feel it.
- Say it a total of three times (if you can).
- Continue this exercise for seven days.

In your journal, reflect on the following questions:
- How did you feel after doing the exercise?
- What thoughts came up for you?
- Was it harder than you thought? Easier?
- What did you learn about yourself?

As you love yourself more and more and appreciate the divinity that is who you are, you'll begin to identify more with your Soulful self and less with your ego. And with that will come a new freedom, a new life, a happier future.

CHAPTER 4

Party Twins

You are unique, and if that is not fulfilled, then something
wonderful has been lost.

~ Martha Graham

W here are the margarita glasses, Ellen? I need a drink!" I
was in my friend's kitchen, helping her set up the buffet
and drinks for a football party.

"They're in the cabinet above the fridge. Do you need a
ladder?"

"Very funny, Ellen. I'm six foot two with these cowboy
boots on. So, who's coming to watch the game?"

Ellen was dumping a huge bag of ice into the ice chest she
had loaded with beer.

"Mostly people from my office, and a couple of guys you've
met before," she shouted.

I arranged the margarita glasses on the tray with a bowl
of lime slices and opened the container of salt. "Ever since my

divorce was finalized last month, it seems like all my friends have disappeared."

"What am I, chopped liver?" she asked.

"I meant my married friends. It's like they think I'm contagious or something."

I picked up a slice of lime and ran it along the rim of a margarita glass, dipped the rim in the salt, and filled the glass with Ellen's famous margarita concoction.

"Well, you can stand here and look at what was, or you can decide to have some fun," she replied.

"You're right," I said. "I've moved over twenty times and changed schools so often, I can't even remember them all. I certainly know how to adapt and make new friends."

We finished the food preparation and walked into the living room to relax and wait on the guests. Ellen turned on the television and was about to change the channel when I yelled, "Wait, that's a commercial for the new movie, *Twins*, with Arnold Schwarzenegger and Danny DeVito."

As we watched the commercial, Ellen laughed and said, "Oh my gosh, that's hilarious. Humongous, muscle-bound Schwarzenegger and dinky DeVito are supposed to be twins? We've got to go see that movie!"

The idea that fraternal twins separated at birth could be so different in looks and personality and have such different perspectives on life because of their experiences gave me a crazy idea.

"Ellen, you're going to think I'm nuts, but what if I pretend I'm my twin tonight?"

"What? You are nuts!" she replied. "Why would you want to be your twin? I don't get it."

Ellen knew I had grown up as a military brat and had lived in different parts of the world. Some years we moved once or twice or even three times. Each move meant adapting to a different school, a different culture, and sometimes learning a new language.

It was always difficult and upsetting to leave behind friends, especially since we knew we would never see each other again. My friends and I tried writing letters to keep in touch, but after a couple of moves, the letters never found me again.

But there was also an upside to constantly moving. I was given the freedom to recreate myself. With each move came a new opportunity to change how I presented myself to the world. I had no history with my new community, so it was easier to change. And since I knew I would be moving within a year or so, even if my new persona was a disaster, I could hold out until the next move and start from scratch in a new town.

Now that I was moving on once again, I realized I had an opportunity to reexamine who I was and who I was becoming.

"I just want to be myself, Ellen. I don't want to be the depressed, angry woman who just got divorced. I'm tired of hiding my personality, of playing small, of trying to please others.

"So, here's my idea. Since a couple of the guys have already met me, what if I pretend to be my own twin? Your friends know me as Kathy, so for tonight I'll be Katie. And since I'm dressed in my country dancing clothes and not in my usual business suit, it will be easier to convince them."

"Okay, but what do you plan to do? I'm still confused," she said.

"I simply plan on having fun. I plan to be myself without editing my words or actions to impress, please, or pacify others. At this point, I don't have anything to lose. So, will you play along?"

"This I gotta see. But what do you want me to do?" she asked.

"Just go along with whatever I say, and try not to laugh."

As the guests began to arrive, Ellen introduced me as Katie, and we both tried to keep a straight face. Then David arrived, one of Ellen's friends whom I had met before.

"Hey, David, meet Kathy's twin sister, Katie. She's here from Houston."

David looked at me, and before he could think too long about it, I said, "So nice to meet you," and gave him a hug. If he had any doubts, they quickly vanished because Kathy rarely hugged anyone. She was diplomatic and professional.

"I didn't know Kathy had a twin. So, where is she?" David asked.

"She's at her apartment. She's still bummed about the divorce and didn't feel like coming. Would you like something to drink?" I asked. "The beer's in the ice chest and the frozen margarita machine is on the buffet table. Help yourself."

Once most of the guests had arrived and were watching the football game in the living room, I motioned for Ellen to meet me in the kitchen. "Okay, so far so good," I said. "Your other friend that knows me didn't show, so David's the only one I'm worried about."

Ellen said, "You know, I was thinking about how funny this is. You're pretending to be someone you are, instead of someone you're not."

"It is a bit crazy how far from myself I've wandered. But, right now, the someone I am wants to go watch the game."

As we entered the living room, David was saying, "You know, Coach Landry tied the NFL record held by Lambeau this year. He's coached twenty-nine consecutive seasons with the same team."

Suddenly, I heard myself say, "He may never break that record at the rate he's going this season. Twelve losses and two wins. This is turning out to be their worst record since 1960!"

David looked at me as if I was from Mars. "Well, I wasn't expecting that! Your sister doesn't seem interested in football." Then he smiled and said, "At least the Cowboys are beating the Redskins right now. We can always hope."

"Yep, even after ten losses in a row, there's always hope," I replied.

Throughout the game, I cheered the Cowboys on when they made great plays, yelled at them when they fumbled, and found myself standing next to the television drawing plays I thought they should have made on the screen with my finger. When the Cowboys won, we all went crazy, cheering and yelling and jumping up and down as if they had just won the Super Bowl.

After the game, we all headed out to Gruene Dance Hall to hear some of the best live music in Texas. David offered to drive me, since he was still under the impression I had flown in from Houston and didn't have a car.

When I turned to look for Ellen, she had already gotten into a pickup truck with some other friends. I thought, *What the heck, the worst that can happen is that he finds out I've been playing a trick on him and he gets mad and walks away.* It wouldn't be the first time someone walked out on me.

It was a forty-minute drive, so he turned on the radio, and we talked about what kind of music we liked. Then Willie Nelson's song, "Blue Eyes Crying in the Rain," came on, and we both sang it together, badly. For most of the drive I asked him about his life and his dreams. Luckily, we arrived at Gruene Hall before he had a chance to ask me too many questions.

As we walked toward the dance hall, David said, "You're a lot more fun than your sister. She takes everything so seriously. It's funny how twins can be so different."

Before I had a chance to respond, the bouncer at the door asked for our identification. As he handed them back to us, he said, "Thank you, David. Thanks, Kathy."

David grabbed the driver's license from my hand, looked at the picture, looked at me and said, "What! You're Kathy? Well, I just stuck my foot in my mouth. Why the charade?"

"Actually, David, today's the day I stopped playing charades."

ᘓᘓᘓ

Something More

As a child raised in the military and constantly moving from place to place, I would try to change my personality to fit in so others would love and accept me. It was like playing a never-ending game of charades. But, no matter how hard I tried to please others, I never felt like I belonged.

As an adult, I continued to play the game because my early conditioning and programming told me that who I really was was not good enough. And I'd been pretending so long to be who I was not that I didn't even know myself any more.

I believed my personality was who I was. That if I found the right persona, I'd finally get the love and acceptance I was searching for.

What I didn't understand is that our personality is NOT who we are! Our personality is our creation, an aspect of ourselves we present to the world. And, it changes from one moment to the next according to the role we are playing and depending on the circumstances and people we are interacting with.

For example, have you ever noticed that at home you have a certain personality and at work your personality is completely different? Or that the way you act around your parents is different than how you act around your friends? Or that your personality with your female friends is very different than your personality with your male friends?

So, if you are not your personality, who are you? You are the *something more* you've been searching for. You are a soul, a spiritual, vibrational being in a human body having a human experience. Your soul is the embodiment of love. It provides the avenue through which Spirit can reach you. It is the link between Spirit and your personality. Your soul knows the part you are here to play in the Divine plan for humanity. It is eternal.

✎✎✎

Something for You

At the Super Bowl party, I was pretending to be my twin so I could stop pretending to be someone I wasn't. For one day, I simply wanted to have fun without the need to please anyone or live up to anyone else's expectations. It was the beginning of my journey back to self-love. This experience was an alignment of my personality with my soul, my true self.

I realized that whatever people think of me is about the image they have of me, and that image isn't me. It's a projection based on their own beliefs and perspectives. And in the same way, what I think of others is based on my perspective. The truth is, I have no idea what is going on in their world or what they are thinking or feeling.

There's great freedom in realizing you don't have to rule your life according to other people's opinions. And there's less pain and drama because you stop taking what others do and say so personally. The only opinion that matters is your opinion of you.

Let's return to your journal to answer the following questions:

- Where in your life have you been playing charades, hiding your true self to please or appease others?
- If you didn't care what others thought about you, what would you be doing differently in your life?
- What is one opinion or judgment you have of yourself that you would like to change?

- What is one step you could take today to begin making that change?

You are unique! There has never been another like you and there will never, ever be another like you. You have something special to offer this world that no one else can. Shine your light bright, and share your uniqueness with the world. We need you! That's why you're here.

Challenge

Complete the following sentences:

One unique thing about me is _____.

What I love about my unique quality is _____.

Another reason I love this about me is _____.

Say this aloud to yourself every morning for one week. Journal about what awareness came up for you by doing this exercise.

CHAPTER 5

War and Pieces

*Are you in my dream or am I in yours—or are we all
trapped in some bizarre combination of each other's
personal version of events?*
~ Deepak Chopra, *Book of Secrets*

I've always wanted to ride in a limousine. I used to fantasize about sipping champagne in the back seat while someone chauffeured me around town. And here I am, riding through the streets of San Antonio in a black limo, except I'm not drinking champagne. Today is my father's funeral. It's March, and the rain is pouring down outside. The wind is blowing so hard it's whistling through the closed car windows.

I feel detached from the scene around me, like a spectator watching a play from the front row but not taking part in the action. All I hear is the hum of voices. Do I know these people? There are my mother, my sisters and brother, and my aunt and uncle. But they seem like strangers to me now. Have they changed that much in three years, or have I?

The chauffeur has no idea where he's going. The military cemetery is the other direction. Why don't men ever ask for directions when they're lost?

I've feared this day my entire life. Even as a child, I lived in constant fear of losing my father. He was always going away on missions for the military. We never knew where he was or when he'd be back. Sometimes he was gone a week, sometimes a year or more. Each time he left, I wondered if I would ever see him again.

I remember when I was about eight years old, we were living in Illinois and my father was on a long mission. One day, my mother was in the kitchen washing dishes when suddenly she simply froze. She wasn't moving at all. She just kept staring out of the kitchen window that faced the front of our house. Two men in military uniforms were coming up the sidewalk. That usually meant only one thing: something bad had happened to my father.

I think I held my breath the whole time they talked with my mother. When the men left, she told me they had only come to visit my father, and they hadn't known he was on a tour of duty. The intensity of the situation was too much for me. I quietly slipped into the bathroom and threw up.

Now, I can't believe this rain. What a day for a funeral. Why did I wear high heels? They're going to sink into the mud. Sandwiched in the back seat between my two sisters and crammed in with other family, I feel trapped. I should have ridden up front with the chauffeur and let my brother sit back here. I'm not even near a door!

Where is this guy going? He's been driving in circles. I'd say something, but it would just give my family more ammunition for criticizing me. I can hear them now: "Don't listen to Kathy; she couldn't find her way to the bathroom without a compass." Why are my mother and sisters criticizing me at a time like this? They even had to make negative comments about my appearance. What does the color of my hair have to do with anything?

My family stopped talking to me over three years ago. They couldn't bear to be around me because I spoke the truth, which they couldn't face at the time: Our family was a lie. Alcohol ruled our home, not love and not affection. I wasn't willing to live the lie any longer, so they had to make a choice. They did. They chose to live in denial.

Sometimes I feel so alone, so alienated. I'm reminded of a line I once read by Dorothy Wordsworth: "One only leaf upon the top of a tree—the sole remaining leaf—danced round and round like a rag blown by the wind." Sometimes it's been hard to hang on and not give up. But I do. I know this tree, this family tree, is not dead. It's only dormant, waiting for a change in season.

My new husband, Mark, is riding in the car behind us. This is the first time he's met my whole family since our recent wedding. He's sitting up front with my brother's pretty girlfriend. I don't like it. She's such a flirt.

No, she's not. I'm just feeling insecure. Being around my family always makes me feel insecure. Sitting in this car with them is suffocating me. If this guy doesn't hurry up and find his way to the cemetery, I'll go crazy!

It's hard to believe he's really gone. My father has escaped death so many times. He was just seventeen, fighting in the Korean War, when he was shot in the face. For that he got a medal—the Purple Heart. When he recovered from his injuries, the Army sent him back to the front, and he was captured and held as a prisoner of war. He somehow escaped, saving the lives of other men as well. He received medals for that too.

But all the medals in the world couldn't erase the horrors he had suffered, so he drank to ease his pain. He was an alcoholic before I was born, and in the end, it killed him. Or, I should say it killed his body. His spirit died a long time ago; the war took care of that.

We're going to be late to the funeral. My dad hated being late. Even now, I can imagine the red spot in the middle of his forehead growing with his anger. But I don't have to fear him anymore, do I?

How am I going to get through this? Finally, my brother is giving the chauffeur directions. We're almost there. Through the rain streaming down the car window, I can see the cemetery with thousands of rows of white tombstones, all lined up like soldiers standing at attention.

We're the last ones to arrive. As we exit the limousine, the rain is coming down so hard it stings when it hits my face. The heels of my shoes are sinking in this stupid mud.

Where is my husband? I can't find him. It looks like I'll have to go through this alone. I don't want to sit next to my mother. I'll get sucked into her grief and know that somehow this is my fault. Good, my brother sat next to her.

Everyone is staring at us. I wonder what they're thinking. Do they know the truth about our family? The coffin seems unreal. I feel like I'm looking through one of those 3D viewers where the picture looks real enough to touch, but it's only an illusion. The military chaplain is giving his generic speech—something about life, liberty, and country. Oh no! The honor guard is lining up to give the twenty-one-gun salute.

BANG!

BANG!

BANG!

Each shot is vibrating through my body, echoing in my ears, breaking down my self-control. A flood of tears streams down my face. A man in formal military dress begins to play "Taps" on his bugle. This song is so slow, so sad, so final. I don't think I can stand this.

The honor guard is folding the flag that was draped over Dad's coffin. Why do they fold it in the shape of a triangle? Solemnly, with great formality, they hand it to Mom. I guess she'll add it to her collection. She's got one from her father's burial and one from each of her two brothers' burials. They all served their country. Wonderful, now she has four neatly folded flags and no family.

I thought funerals brought families closer together. Not ours. It seems impossible that we could be more emotionally distant from one another than we already are. I try to hug Mom and comfort her, but she's hard and stiff. She's playing the brave little soldier, just like Dad always taught us to.

Where's my husband? There he is, standing by himself in the rain. He's soaked. No one offered him the shelter of their umbrella. It's just as well; there's always a price to pay when you get involved with my family.

Why did my mother just hit Dad's coffin with her fist? I can't believe she did that. Is she angry at him for dying, or is she mad at him because he didn't try harder to keep their marriage together? She's probably mad at him for a lot of things. I am. They never talked. Now, it's too late.

Everyone's leaving. I wish I didn't have to get back into that limousine. Just a little longer and I'll be back in the real world. *I can handle this. I can handle this. I can handle this.*

I struggled through three long years of therapy, soul-searching, and forgiveness to work through my problems and to regain my self-respect. But it was worth it. Through God's grace and love, I have a second chance for a happy life. Maybe someday I will feel strong enough to face my family again without the fear of being pulled back into the pain of our past. But today is not that day.

I can't believe this guy is lost again! I do not want to ride around in this limousine. I want out of here! My brother is giving him directions again. Oh, great! Now the road is blocked. Why is the driver just sitting here? Can't he see the detour? Can't he find his way around this roadblock? All he has to do is follow the other cars. Why isn't he moving?

I want to go home…

ඉඉඉ

Something More

Have you ever tried to discuss a past event from childhood with a sibling or parent only to discover they either don't remember it at all or their version barely resembles yours? It's because our reality is true only for us; we are the creators of our stories. And as the creators, we bring to our version perceptions colored by our past experiences.

I wrote this chapter, War and Pieces, in 1992, soon after the death of my father when my feelings were still raw from too much psychotherapy, too much thinking, too much analyzing of the past.

I was looking at the story of my dad's funeral through the eyes of abandonment. I was grieving not only the loss of my father but also the loss of a dream. A dream that I might one day hear the words, "I love you," from my father.

The anger I was feeling knocked reality out of focus and prevented me from seeing any good that might have been present, any kindness that might have been extended. My personality (ego) was trying to protect me from pain because I couldn't face the fear that I was unlovable.

It wasn't until many years later that I realized the core cause of anger is lack of self-worth. And changing external circumstances was not the solution. Trying to win the love and approval of others would not heal the pain. It is not what we say or do that matters. Because love is not earned through good behavior and meeting other people's needs.

It is through the alignment of your personality with your soul that you magnetize love and all good things to yourself. It is the essence of the love that you are, the love that you feel, that draws people to you and keeps them there.

All healing is a journey of self-love.

ℰℰℰ

Something for You

Healing begins with understanding that ALL emotions are a gift. Emotions are simply energy in motion (e-motion). And each emotion has its own frequency of vibration. The thoughts we think create our emotions, and the longer we focus on a thought, the stronger the emotion becomes.

Whether you experience joy and love or anger and fear, they all have a message for you. Emotions are communication from the soul, letting you know whether your thoughts are in alignment with your desires or not. Simply put, when you feel good, you are in alignment. When you feel bad, you are not. Acknowledging and accepting ALL your emotions is the first step toward wholeness. Without that knowledge, you cannot change.

As long as we continue to tell stories from the ego's perspective, we remain a victim of circumstances. We feel powerless, unloved, and unworthy. We have no energy because these are lower vibrational emotions.

The good news is, we get to choose how we tell the stories of our life. We are the creator living in our creation. If we have a story from the past that doesn't feel good, we have the opportunity to look at it through the eyes of love. To do that, we must first bridge the gap between the personality and the soul.

If you're ready to experience a new, better feeling version of an event from your life, you will need your journal and a comfortable chair for this exercise.

- Sit comfortably in your chair with your feet on the ground.
- Think of a past event you would like to feel better about.
- Notice what emotions come up for you when you think about the event. Where are you feeling them in your body?
- Next, place one hand on your solar plexus (above your belly button, below the ribs) and one hand on your heart. Your solar plexus is your power center where your innate wisdom resides. Your breath is your Spirit. It is through your breath that you can bridge the gap between the personality and the soul.
- Close your eyes and relax your shoulders. Take slow, deep belly breaths in and out through your nose. Your belly should expand on the inhale and contract on the exhale.
- Imagine you are breathing loving presence into your body on the inhale and expanding love throughout your body on the exhale. The slower you breathe, the more you connect with the soul.
- As you calm your emotions and quiet your mind, imagine your protective personality is standing before you. Thank

your personality for all the good things it is trying to do for you. Show your personality your current plans and goals of blending with your soul and expanding your ability to love.

- Ask your personality if it will work with your soul to help you see the gifts in the past event that you would like to feel better about. Once your personality agrees, imagine a bridge between your personality and your soul.
- Imagine your soul and personality meeting in the center of the bridge. As they connect, they blend into a symbol of light. Take this symbol into your heart and blend with it.
- Take a deep breath in. Feel this new, beautiful light within you as your soul and personality align. When you are ready, slowly open your eyes and come back into the room.

In your journal:
- Rewrite the story of the event from the perspective of love and alignment.
- What did this past experience teach you about yourself? About your strengths? About your resilience?
- How did your past experience help you grow?
- What emotions do you feel now that you can see the gifts in this experience?

In the future, any time you're tempted to tell your old story, stop and breathe. And share your better-feeling story instead. For as you turn your pain into purpose, you not only increase your capacity for self-love, but you also give hope to others.

CHAPTER 6

The Secret Revealed

The first step is to ask. Make a command to the Universe. Let the
Universe know what you want.

~ Lisa Nichols, quoted in *The Secret*

I can't believe after all these years I can't figure this out!" It's nine o'clock in the morning, and I'm standing in the self-help book aisle at Barnes and Noble, talking to myself and scanning the shelves for an answer. I'm searching for one more book that might offer a clue.

My bookshelves at home are filled with so many self-help, new age, and spiritual books that during a recent dinner party at our home, a neighbor asked if I were a therapist. I even have them shelved in alphabetical order by author for easy reference—everything from Martha Beck, Julia Cameron, and Jack Canfield to Joe Vitale, Marianne Williamson, and Zig Ziglar.

Every book offered me more insight, more awareness, and a deeper understanding of who I am and why I do the things

I do, but a piece of the puzzle was still missing for me. With everything I'd read, learned, and worked through over the years, why wasn't I happy?

"I know there's something I'm missing, what is it?"

"Excuse me, were you talking to me?" a young man asked.

I looked up to see other people in the aisle were staring at me.

"Oops! Sorry. I didn't realize I said that out loud," I replied and quickly exited the self-help section.

Sighing, I thought, *I'll just go buy a Janet Evanovich mystery novel. Maybe the antics of Stephanie Plum, the bungling bounty hunter, and her spandex-wearing sidekick, Lula, will distract me for a while.*

As I pulled *Ten Big Ones* off the shelf, a small book that had been wedged in next to it fell to the floor. I reached to pick it up and thought it looked small for a mystery novel.

The book jacket looked like an old piece of parchment paper with script handwriting and a wax seal. It was a book by Rhonda Byrne titled *The Secret*.

I turned to the back cover and read, "You hold in your hands a great secret…" I still thought it was a mystery novel, but as I continued reading, my heart started racing, and it felt like someone was poking me in the chest.

The hair stood up on the back of my neck and tears came to my eyes as I read the words "you will come to know how you can have, be, or do anything you want. You will come to know who you really are. You will come to know the true magnificence that awaits you in life."

Was this the answer I was looking for?

I immediately went to the bookstore cafe, ordered my grande mocha and a brownie cookie, found a seat in the corner of the cafe, and started reading.

As I read each chapter, my heart beat faster. But this might be partly attributed to the caffeine high from the coffee and brownie.

In less than two hours, I had finished the book and felt like Dorothy in the *Wizard of Oz* when she pulled back the curtain and learned the truth. The ruby slippers, the secret, the missing piece of the puzzle I'd been searching for, was the Law of Attraction: Like attracts like.

I wasn't happy because I kept focusing on all the bad things that had happened in my life, so my thoughts were creating more unwanted things.

Thoughts become things.
~ Mike Dooley

I finally had the answer I was looking for. Or so I thought.

Weeks passed and the initial excitement of discovering the Law of Attraction became muted by everyday life. I did my best to think positive thoughts. I created affirmations about what I wanted and said them every day. I kept a journal and wrote down the details of my desires. But, little changed. My relationships, my finances, my business were still mediocre at best.

One day, while sitting at the kitchen table discussing a book project we were collaborating on, my friend from India asked, in her proper British accent, "What's new with you? You seem a bit down today."

"I'm just frustrated, Vasu. I recently read a book called *The Secret* and was eager to make changes in my life, yet I haven't been able to. I'm doing the things they suggest, but something seems to be blocking me."

"Is that the book that talks about the Law of Attraction?" she asked.

"Yes," I replied. "Have you read it?"

"No, but I've heard about it. I'm reading another book that might be similar."

Vasu picked it up and handed it to me. I read the front cover: *Law of Attraction: The Basics of the Teachings of Abraham.* I immediately assumed the book was about the patriarch Abraham of the Old Testament, and having studied various religions and versions of the Bible, I didn't feel inspired to read it.

"Thanks," I said as I handed the book back to her. "Maybe I'll look at it later."

...there is not another who attracts into your experience that which you are getting—you are doing it all.
~ Esther and Jerry Hicks/Abraham, *The Law of Attraction*

A week passed, and I found myself standing in a long checkout line at Barnes and Noble, balancing another stack of self-help books. Next to me was a tall stand of boxed CDs. Some were music, and some were books. As I glanced at the titles, one stood out for me: *Law of Attraction: The Basics of the Teachings of Abraham,* by Esther and Jerry Hicks.

This time I read the back of the box and realized it was not about the biblical Abraham, as I had originally believed. The book promised that it would show me how to make the Law of Attraction work to my advantage and to take the guesswork out of daily living, so I added it to my pile.

As soon as I got into my car, I wrestled the bulletproof plastic wrapper off the CD box by stabbing it with my car keys. Then I slipped the first disc into my CD player, pushed the play button, and headed home.

As I listened, I realized the reason positive thinking, affirmations, and journaling produced little change in my life was because I had not been paying attention to my emotions. Even though I thought I was focused on what I wanted, I was actually focused on its absence. How do I know? Because I was feeling doubt and fear. Doubt and fear that my desires would manifest.

We can't achieve our desires while feeling negative emotion. We can't attract prosperity if we feel poor. We can't attract love if we feel unlovable. We can't attract thin if we feel fat. It defies the Law of Attraction.

The missing piece of the puzzle was understanding that my emotions were the indicator of the vibrational signal I was sending out to the Universe. And the Universe was responding, not to my words or desires, but to my vibration.

This understanding of how our thoughts and feelings create our reality began my journey down the yellow brick road, changing my perception of life forever.

Toto, I have a feeling we're not in Kansas anymore.
~ Dorothy, in L. Frank Baum's *The Wonderful Wizard of Oz*

ଔଔଔ

Something More

Once I understood the Universal Laws and how they operate, I realized that if I could dream it, then the Universe/God/Source/ All That Is could deliver it to me. My work was simply to ask and allow it in.

In the bookstore, I was asking the Universe for guidance to information that would help me create a life filled with joy, fun, and adventure. But I began my search feeling frustrated, so I couldn't easily find what I was looking for, which made me more frustrated. I was a vibrational match to frustrating things, so that's all I could receive.

Once I released resistance by shifting my focus to something I enjoyed, mystery novels, I shifted from feeling frustration to feeling eager with anticipation. I was now a vibrational match to my desire. And even though I was in the mystery section, the self-help book I was "asking" for was where it needed to be for me to find it. The Universe threw the book on the floor in front of me!

Likewise, when I visited my friend, Vasu, I was frustrated that *The Secret* didn't seem to have the answers to all my questions. So, when Vasu offered me the book, *Law of Attraction*, I pushed it away. Later, standing in line at the bookstore, I felt hopeful that one of the books I was holding had some answers.

That vibration of hopefulness gave me another opportunity to receive what I was asking for, and I found it in the CD rack.

I imagine you can remember a similar experience in your own life when you wanted something and it appeared from an unlikely source or out of the blue. It always happens in a moment of surrender, often when you are focused on something else that makes you feel good.

ఴఴఴ

Something for You

Do you understand the process of asking? Focused thought creates an emotional vibration relative to the subject of your attention. That is your asking. You get what you think about whether you want it or not.

The Universe is always responding to your vibration. Think of the range of human emotions as a frequency scale. Joy, freedom, empowerment, love, and appreciation are at the top of the scale with the highest vibrational frequency. And fear, grief, depression, and powerlessness are at the bottom of the scale with the lowest vibration. Your emotions are indicators of your point of attraction.

When we ask, we are often in the vibration of lack because we notice that we don't yet have that thing we want. To receive our desire, we must first shift our vibration to one of expectation and eagerness.

Sometimes it is easier to shift our vibration to a higher frequency by focusing on those things that are unrelated to our desire. For example, if we are wanting more money and are feeling the lack of money, it is easier to focus on another aspect of life that is joyful: puppies, butterflies, nature.

Whenever we focus on something with appreciation and love, we are sending out a high vibrational frequency. The Law of Attraction responds by magnetizing those things we desire that are a vibrational match. It's like having the secret keypad code that opens the door to all your desires.

Likewise, whenever we send out lower vibrational frequencies like doubt, anger, jealousy, fear, and frustration, the Law of Attraction also responds by magnetizing those things that are a vibrational match.

Deliberately creating a life you love is about deliberate vibration. By paying attention to your emotions, you have instant feedback on whether your thoughts are moving you closer to or farther from your desire.

To be a deliberate creator, we must be aware of our emotions. Emotions are a physiological event that lasts ninety seconds in the body. Yes, only one minute and a half. So why does anger over an event seem to last for hours, days, and sometimes years? Because we keep the story alive in our present by focusing on it. Wherever our focus goes, energy flows.

Within seventeen seconds of focusing on something, you activate a vibration within you that begins attracting other thoughts that match. If you stay focused on any thought for as little as sixty-eight seconds, the vibration is powerful enough to begin a manifestation.

When you repeatedly return to the thought, over time it becomes a dominant thought that runs on autopilot until you change it. That's why it's important to become aware of your emotions and use them as your guidance system.

Your mission this week, should you choose to accept it, is to pay close attention to your emotions and make them your ally.

- Notice if the emotion feels good or bad.
- If the emotion feels good, continue focusing on whatever thought created the emotion and any other thoughts that feel the same for at least sixty-eight seconds. This is the length of time it takes for the vibration you're offering to begin to manifest other experiences that feel good.
- If the emotion feels bad, DO NOT continue to focus on the thought that created the emotion. Instead, just be with the emotion without judgement and notice how the feeling dissipates within ninety seconds.
- Notice how what you're thinking and feeling and what manifests in your life is always a vibrational match.
- Write any observations from this exercise in your journal.

CHAPTER 7

I See the Light

*Having and enjoying anything begins with honoring
what we already have.*

~ Unknown

Your home's on fire! Quick! Tell me what to rescue," I said with urgency.

She laughed and answered, "That chair and ottoman, the blue glass vase, the painting of the ocean my mother painted, the blue-and-green rug I bought in Turkey, and the aqua-and-green Italian wine bottles."

"Good choices, Sarah," I replied. This is my favorite question to ask my clients when redecorating their home. They will intuitively choose their favorite things if they don't have too much time to think about it.

"Are those demijohns antiques?" I asked.

"What are demijohns?"

"The Italian wine bottles," I replied. "Typically, the wavy glass bottles were wrapped in wicker to act as a sort of cushion while in transit on long, bumpy wagon rides. Most antiques don't have the wicker because it would have deteriorated over time."

"Oh, no, I just bought these at Anthropologie," she replied.

"Well, you have a great eye. And I promise to put the items you saved back into this room. Do I have your permission to move other pieces out and bring in others from your other rooms?"

"I guess that would be okay."

I always find it interesting that clients call me because they are tired of their home and say they want change, yet they don't want to move anything.

"Sarah, I'm here to give you a new perspective, to help you see your home with fresh eyes. Anything we do can be changed back if you don't like it. As we discussed on the phone, I ask that you live with the new arrangement for one week, and if you decide you want to change it back, I will do it free of charge. Are you willing to give it a try?"

"Yes, of course. I don't know why I'm so resistant. This house has been driving me crazy. I've had it arranged this way for so long, I can't imagine it any other way."

"Most of us are resistant to change because we fear the future might be worse than the present. So, we hang on to what we have, keep things the way they are.

"What's exciting about rearranging furniture that you already have is that it's a safe way to open to new things and learn to trust and have faith in yourself and others. When you apply it in one area of your life, it expands into others."

"I get it. There's nothing serious going on here. I'm just moving furniture around," she said.

"Right. When you donate those things you no longer have use for, you're creating space or a void for the new to come into your life. So, let's get started by clearing the room."

We quickly cleared the living room of everything except the larger pieces of furniture. As I rearranged the seating, Sarah began telling me all the reasons she thought the new arrangement wouldn't work.

"I know it's hard to imagine what the finished room will look like, but let's wait until all of the pieces are in place and then see what you think."

In a matter of minutes, I can see a project completed simply by scanning the room and rearranging the space in my mind. "Okay, Sarah, now that we have the furniture in place, let's go look under your bed."

"What?" she asked.

"I noticed you have a dust ruffle around your bed. One thing I've learned after rearranging and redecorating hundreds of homes is that the good stuff is under the bed."

A lot of clients will purchase something they love, bring it home and like many things that they could do for themselves to improve their lives, it gets shoved under the bed because they don't take the time to make the change.

As we walked into her bedroom, she said, "That's so weird. I do have stuff hidden under the bed, but I don't remember what's under here."

I held up the dust ruffle as Sarah reached underneath and pulled out a large, long package wrapped in brown paper, a box full of seashells and a bag of sand, a wood sign with the words *Beach Cottage* painted on it, four blue-and-white striped pillow covers, and two green metal lanterns with candles.

"My stuff is such a hodgepodge, and nothing really goes together," she said as she tore the brown paper wrapping off the two old wooden shutters covered in layers of peeling paint. "I don't know what I'm going to do with these, but I just had to buy them."

"Actually, Margaret, you have a very definite style," I replied.

"What do you mean?"

As I held up the *Beach Cottage* sign, a smile slowly spread across her face. "Oh my gosh! It's been right in front of me, and I didn't even realize it."

"It's just that you've been buying one piece at a time, but never pulled everything out together to see the bigger picture. And remember the items you saved from the imaginary fire: your mother's painting of the ocean, the blue glass vase, the blue-and-green rug, and the glass wine bottles? You intuitively know that your style is beach cottage, but your belief that you didn't have a style blocked you from seeing the obvious."

"I'm so excited about changing my living room now. I'm ready to get rid of everything that doesn't work with the beach cottage style," Sarah said as we moved her forgotten treasures into the staging area we had set up in her dining room.

"Let's start by creating a focal point by hanging your mother's ocean painting over your fireplace," I said. "I'll hang the painting while you put the striped covers on the throw pillows and arrange them on your white sofa."

A few minutes later, as Sarah was placing candles in the green metal lanterns, she asked, "What are you doing with those shutters?"

"Well, since you didn't like your old glass coffee table, I'm going to screw the shutters side-by-side to the old table legs and then place the glass on top."

"I would never have thought of that. I love it!"

A couple hours later, the transformation was complete. As Sarah and I stepped back to look at the room, tears welled up in her eyes. "I feel like I've come home," she said. "And everything I needed was here with me all along."

There are two kinds of requests: those made by your personality, and those made by your soul.

~ Sanaya Roman

On my drive home, the joyful feeling from helping my client quickly changed to frustration and confusion. "Why is this so hard?" I yelled to God.

For months, I had been contemplating closing my business to spend time writing. But each time I worked with a client and realized the effect my work had on their lives, I doubted my decision to write.

What if I gave up a growing business that I enjoyed, only to discover that I'm not a good writer? Does what I have to say really matter to anyone but me?

"Give me a sign!" I yelled as I slapped the dashboard of my car. "I don't know what to do!"

Suddenly, a red pickup truck sped past me on my left and the driver lost control, drove over the median, hit a giant light pole, and skidded into oncoming traffic. I looked up through my sunroof and saw the light pole coming down above me, and I thought, *Well, this is it; I'm done.*

Everything shifted to slow motion, and I had the sensation of floating in a protective bubble. Strangely, I felt no fear.

I looked in my rearview mirror as the light pole crashed to the ground in a loud explosion behind me. Cars were swerving off the road and crashing into each other trying to avoid the metal beam that now blocked the road.

I drove in a daze, trying to make sense of what just happened. Wondering if I was really alive. It felt as if someone else was driving my car, like I was in a dream.

I pulled off to the side of the road, and reality hit me. My hands shook uncontrollably as tears streamed down my face. Why am I still here? What if I had died? What would I regret?

In that moment, I decided I wanted to make a bigger difference in this world, I wanted to uplift others, and I wanted to write a book.

Margaret's words echoed in my ears. "I feel like I've come home, and everything I needed was here with me all along."

ᘓᘓᘓ

Something More

Just like my client, I was afraid to step outside my comfort zone and try something new; yet my soul yearned for adventure. God showed me the light, literally.

The reason we hesitate making changes in our lives, whether it's applying for a new job, ending a relationship, or simply redecorating our home is because our subconscious mind makes it hard for us to change. The ego prefers we stay on autopilot to protect us from the unknown. That's why when we disrupt our habits and routines to attempt something new we feel fear.

Our subconscious stores every experience we have in our life and never edits or deletes. Imagine your subconscious is like a closet that holds all your clothing from the day you were born and nothing has ever been removed. And each piece of clothing represents an experience that contains the emotions and perspectives you had at the time you were wearing it.

When you're on autopilot, your ego will choose what you wear today from your subconscious closet, even if it no longer fits. And if you try to step outside your comfort zone to try something new, it will try to convince you that it's not your style, people will laugh, you'll be criticized or judged.

So, how do we claim the *something more* we've been searching for? By living consciously. By living in the present moment. Research shows that we have over sixty thousand thoughts a day and ninety-five percent of those thoughts are subconscious. That means we operate only five percent of our day in a conscious state.

To be the creator of your life, you must live from your authentic self, the soul. Otherwise, your subconscious thoughts will continue to control your life and nothing will change.

ՑՑՑ

Something for You

To live as the authentic self, we must practice present moment awareness. Just the act of consciously choosing to do this next activity will help you connect more deeply to your soul.

- Right now, wherever you are sitting, notice how the chair beneath you feels to your body. Is it soft, hard? Is it comfortable? Do you feel supported?
- Where are your feet? Are they flat on the floor? Tucked underneath you? If you have shoes on, how do the shoes feel? If you are barefoot, are your feet warm or cold?
- How does this book feel in your hands? Is it heavy or light? What does the texture feel like?
- Notice your shoulders. Are they relaxed or tense?
- Pay attention to your breath. Are you breathing slowly or rapidly, deep or shallow, or perhaps you're holding your breath?
- Notice the temperature of the room. What smells do you notice? What sounds?
- If any thoughts pop into your awareness, just notice them without judgement and imagine them floating away on a cloud.

By bringing the attention of your mind onto your body and breath, you create a deeper connection between mind, body, and spirit. Continue to practice present moment awareness each day. Perhaps set a timer on your cell phone to remind you to take a couple minutes, two or three times a day, to focus on the present. By practicing on a consistent basis, you begin to transform your life.

Transformation
Like a butterfly emerging from its chrysalis,
Requires that we shed our old habits,
Patterns and perspectives
To emerge into this world as our authentic self
~Kat Wells

CHAPTER 8

Dyer Intentions

No one else is responsible for your imagination. Anything placed in your imagination and held there ultimately becomes your reality.

~ Wayne Dyer

Dear Dr. Dyer,

A funny thing happened to me on the way to the Maui Writer's Conference, and I wanted to share it with you since you were an unknowing participant in the story.

Over the years, I have read all your books, watched many of your PBS specials, and bought many of your Whole Shebang audio and video offerings. Because of your generous spirit and wisdom, my life has been forever changed. Your teaching has led me to other teachers as well, and one of the most powerful concepts I've come to understand is the Law of Attraction.

Once I understood and accepted that I am the creator of my life, that I am responsible for all of it, that I attract everything to me, I became intentional with my creating, and this is where our story begins.

My husband, Mark, and I were sitting in our living room one evening in August 2007 watching your PBS special, and during the show you mentioned you had moved to Maui. Since I had a trip planned to attend the Maui Writer's Conference the following week, I mentioned to my husband that I wanted to meet you while we were there.

He just rolled his eyes and said, "You don't have time to go to one of his seminars even if he were giving one. Are you planning on trying to call him? How will you get in touch with him?"

I smiled and told him that the *how* wasn't my concern. I just wanted to meet you while I was there.

I did not try to figure out how or when or where we would meet because I knew it would create resistance, and I wanted to allow the Universe to surprise and delight me. Likewise, I did not talk to my husband about it again because even though our lives had dramatically changed for the better in a short amount of time, Mark still wasn't convinced that the Law of Attraction had much to do with it. So, I just imagined and practiced the feeling of it, the fun of it, and the knowing of it.

The following week, on September 22, 2008, we were in Dallas and boarded our connecting flight to Maui. This was our first time to fly first class, and we were excitedly exploring our comfortable seats, pushing buttons, drinking champagne out of real glasses, and observing the other passengers as they were boarding the plane.

Two men were already seated in the front row of the center aisle. One man, who was bald, was rubbing the top of his head, and my husband said, "I notice bald men seem to do that a lot."

I turned to him and said, "It's probably because the air vent is blowing on his head." As I was looking at Mark, his eyes got big, and he started laughing. I asked him, "What's so funny?"

He said, "You got your wish. That bald guy is Wayne Dyer."

I turned to see you standing up to get something out of the overhead compartment. My husband shook his head in disbelief and said, "Well, go say hello."

I was so excited that I couldn't get my seat belt unfastened. My husband reached over and unlatched it. But as I was getting up, the flight attendant instructed me to sit down, put my chair back in the upright position, and buckle my seatbelt.

At one point later in the flight, I made my way up the aisle to introduce myself, but you were sleeping, and I didn't want to intrude. Although I didn't get a chance to speak with you that day, I was just as happy knowing that in less than one month, I was able to manifest an event that would appear to others to be nearly impossible. I was ecstatic. Even more important, my husband's belief shifted, and he began to understand that we truly do create our own reality.

So, thank you for sharing your wisdom and for inspiring me to take responsibility for creating the life of my dreams.

Someday I know we will meet face-to-face. For now, I'm thrilled that my husband is currently focusing on his heart's desire with a new perspective. Life is good.

With Love and Appreciation,
Kat

P.S. Sorry about the "bald guy" thing.

ৎৎৎ

Something More

In his book, *Inspiration, Your Ultimate Calling*, Dr. Dyer suggests to "Monitor your thoughts for any that put bonds on your ability to manifest." In other words, since we have no limits on what we can create, it is simply our thoughts and beliefs that allow or disallow its manifestation.

That's why I chose to stop discussing my desire to meet Dr. Dyer with my husband. Trying to convince anyone that your desire is attainable will create a wobble in your vibration, which allows the fog of doubt to creep in.

Whatever you are inspired (in-spirit) to create, the Universe/Source/God/All That Is, has the ability to deliver in magical and unexpected ways. You simply must be a vibrational match to your desire. When I wrote the letter to Dr. Dyer, I intended to give it to him at his Celebrate Your Life event. Although I didn't know specifically how I would meet him, I simply focused on my gratitude for his work.

Prior to the event, I kept having dreams of meeting him in a glass elevator going up to the top floor of a building. As we rode the elevator, we could see everyone from the event on the ground floor beneath us as we continued to rise.

It was in the elevator that I gave him the letter, which he received with grace and reverence. It was such a vivid dream and so satisfying that it no longer mattered whether I physically gave it to him. I felt at a soul level he had already received my love and appreciation.

Not long after my dream and just two months before the conference, Dr. Wayne Dyer left this earthly realm on August 29, 2015. When I heard the news, it occurred to me that the elevator dream was a gift of Spirit. And each time I rode the elevator at the Celebrate Your Life event, I smiled in remembrance and appreciation for all that he added to my life.

ᘓᘓᘓ

Something for You

My pure and powerful desire to express appreciation magnetized an abundance of wonderful opportunities at the event. Not only new friendships that continue to this day, but also new mentors to help me on my path of living from my authentic self.

I spent a full day with Dr. Bruce Lipton, author of *Biology of Belief*, a renowned cell biologist who taught me how the cells of our body are affected by our thoughts.

I also met Neale Donald Walsh, author of *Conversations with God,* who shared with me that our feelings are the language of our soul. If I want to know what's true for me, I need to pay attention to my feelings.

And finally, I met my dear friend and teacher, Dr. Sue Morter, the founder of the Morter Institute for BioEnergetics and author of *The Energy Codes.* I spent the day with her and was so inspired by her message of human potentiality that I spent over six years training and traveling with her.

All these opportunities and experiences were a direct response to my high vibration at the event. And my high vibe was created through appreciation. The vibration of appreciation is the most powerful connection between the physical you and your soul. The more you practice gratitude, the more clearly you receive guidance from your soul.

If you're ready for *something more* exciting and inspiring in your life, let's begin with gratitude for what you already have. For this adventure, you'll need your journal and a timer (your cell phone works great for this).

You will be making a list of all the things in your life you are grateful for. Keep the list simple. For example, your list could be: sunshine, butterflies, puppies, car, running water, electricity, and so on.

- Before you begin, relax your neck and shoulders. Take several deep belly breaths and connect with your body.
- Next, set your timer for two minutes.
- In your journal, list all the things you are grateful for.

Keep adding to the list until the timer goes off.

- Notice if this was easy or difficult for you. Did you easily keep adding to your list for the full two minutes or did you struggle?

When I first started keeping a gratitude journal, I could only think of three things to put on my list. It was simply that I had not trained myself to look for the good in my life. As I continued to do the exercise on a consistent basis, my list easily grew.

Just for fun, while I was writing this chapter I completed this exercise, and I came up with forty-three items in two minutes. If I were to set the timer for two more minutes, I could easily come up with forty-three more. We have so much to be grateful for, yet when we are living on autopilot, we miss what is right in front of us because we are not in present moment awareness.

Please don't be discouraged if you struggled with this exercise. Instead, celebrate! Once you strengthen your appreciation muscles, miracles will happen in your life. So be very excited!

If you'd like to flex your appreciation muscles and kick this up a notch, choose one of the items from your list, reset your timer for five minutes, and write all the reasons WHY you are grateful.

For example, if you picked sunshine, you could write: I am so grateful for the sun. It feels so warm and delicious on my skin. It provides energy for plants to grow, which provides food for our planet. I love how it lights our world, how it reflects light off the rain and creates rainbows...

The fun thing about this activity is that after five minutes of focused appreciation, you will feel amazing. And keep an eye out for evidence of your alignment. Something fun and exciting will show up during your day.

CHAPTER 9

When "Why" Means "No"

You are the designer of your destiny; you are the
author of your story.

~ Lisa Nichols

The line was longer than I had expected, and I couldn't see her from where I stood. "Is this the line for Lisa Nichols?" I asked the woman standing in front of me.

"Yes, and it looks like it's going to be a long wait," she replied.

Well, if I had to stand in a long line, Maui was the place to do it. I took a deep breath of the ocean air and looked out over the sands of Wailea Beach. This was my first trip to Hawaii and my first pitch to publishers. It took every ounce of self-control I could muster to keep from jumping up and down with excitement.

I'd spent the last several days in a writing course with Sam Horn to create a proposal for my book *Heart Connections*. Through her processes and guidance, it transformed from a poetry-and-art book into my story of transformation, *War and Pieces*.

Since the manuscript I came with was not the book I'd be presenting, I'd been practicing my pitch every day in front of my hotel room mirror. In fact, there was no book, only the first chapter. And though I didn't yet have a clear vision of the book, I was eager to go through the terrifying process of pitching to publishers and possible rejection.

Like the first time I drove a car, my excitement overrode any fear because I knew moving through the fear was the first step toward freedom.

"There she is!" yelled the woman in front of me.

Our line had moved around the corner of the building, and I could see Lisa Nichols sitting at a table with stacks of books piled high behind her. She was signing copies of *The Secret* and taking her time with each person.

Sitting next to her was Dan Millman with a posterboard of his book, *The Peaceful Warrior*, propped up next to him. There were only three people in his line, and I wondered what he was thinking about the event.

I remember his book being promoted as a fictional story, yet I'd also read somewhere that it was based on his true-life experience. It's a beautiful story, but it had me questioning how much of myself I wanted to share with the public. I still feared the judgment of others and hesitated to share how I had used the Law of Attraction to create massive change in my life. Lisa, on the other hand, was totally transparent.

As the line got shorter, I could clearly see Lisa and noticed how gracious she was with everyone. She took their hands or hugged them, made eye contact, and took time to chat with each person.

When I reached the table, Lisa took my hand in hers and said, "Hello, Beautiful, what's your name?"

"Kathy," I replied. "It's so wonderful to meet you, Lisa. I've read about your program, Motivating the Teen Spirit, and the work you're doing to empower kids and teens. I'm interested in being involved and supporting you. Do you offer training?"

Lisa's smile filled her face. She was still holding my hand as she looked deeply into my eyes and whispered, "Actually, I have a new training program starting up soon. Let me give you my email address, and you can contact me there."

She autographed my book, and as she handed it back to me, she said, "Talk to you soon."

Anytime we are looking outside ourselves for an experience that can only be generated from within—such as approval, recognition, acceptance, or love—we are coming from a mindset of lack.

~ Christy Whitman

Later that day, as I stood in another line waiting to pitch my book to the publishers, I was feeling eager and scared as hell. My issues of unworthiness and inferiority started to rear their ugly heads. My mind began to wander to thoughts of *What if I'm not good enough? What if no one cares about my story?*

"Kathy Wells," a woman's voice called out, jarring me from my ruinous ruminations. "You're up next," she added.

I walked on wobbly legs into the huge conference room, not sure what to expect. The room was filled with tables and publishers and want-to-be authors pitching their books. My insecurities began to intensify, and by the time I reached the table where I was to present my pitch, my mind went blank.

"Just take a deep breath," the publisher offered. "Take your time."

"Thank you," I replied and took a couple of deep breaths and began. "While there are other narrative nonfiction books about life in the military, *War and Pieces* is different. It contradicts the current assumption that 'all is well' if Dad returns home safe from the war."

My emotions bubbled up as I continued. "*War and Pieces* is written from the child's perspective and reveals how war touches the lives of military children, not only in childhood, but forever."

I became so emotional I could barely finish. "It reveals the reality of military family life behind closed doors." Tears started flowing, and it took a great deal of effort to maintain my composure.

"Why do you want to publish this book?" she asked.

"I had such a hard life growing up, and I lived through years of heartache, struggle, and pain. I just want others to learn from my life, so they don't have to struggle like I did."

"Well, I do believe you have a story to tell. And I don't know if you're ready yet. But don't give up. Thank you for your time and for stepping outside your comfort zone to do this. It isn't easy. Good luck."

"Thank you for your time," I said and hurried out the door clutching my manuscript.

Through my tears I could see Sam Horn walking toward me. "So, what happened?" she asked.

I wiped the tears from my eyes and said, "I'm not sure. The publisher asked me why I wanted to publish my book, and I guess my *why* wasn't good enough."

"Well, don't be so hard on yourself. Almost every person here has been working on their book proposal for months. You did yours in three days. That's amazing."

"I don't know why I got so emotional during the interview," I replied. "I guess I was looking for validation."

"No matter what happens today," Sam said, "I want you to remember and to know you are an excellent writer. You have a gift."

"Thank you, Sam. That means a lot coming from you," I replied. "Let's go down to the beach bar. I think I'll order some pupu and a blue Hawaiian. Kind of matches my mood at the moment."

"Lead the way, sister!"

ভ ভ ভ

Something More

There's *something more* to this story than I was capable of recognizing at the time. I wasn't rejected because my "why" wasn't good enough. It was because I was writing from the perspective of the victim rather than the victor. It wasn't my words, but my emotional response that gave the publisher clues that I wasn't ready.

Why did I have such a strong emotional reaction? I was revealing a personal and vulnerable aspect of my life where I still carried shame. I had stepped outside my comfort zone and put myself in a situation to be rejected, and my personality (ego) was screaming, "N-O-O-O-O-O-O!!!"

My emotions were guiding me to the awareness that it was time to challenge the belief that I was unworthy. The discomfort I felt during the interview was temporary and necessary for me to let go of a narrative that was holding me back from living my passion.

I didn't recognize this at first. It wasn't until weeks later during my interview with Lisa Nichols, when I was in the process of joining her team, that I discovered I still carried the core belief that I was unworthy.

Part of the application process was to create a video explaining "Why" I was a good fit for her team and "Why" I was passionate about the project. I was excited to do the video and thought I had done an excellent job. That was until I watched the video.

As the observer, it was clear to me that although my words and intentions came from my true desire to be of service, the emotions I was feeling in the moment told me a different story. I was not yet a vibrational match to my desire because I was still looking for validation of my worthiness from others, from outside myself.

So, I contacted Lisa to thank her for the opportunity and to let her know that I needed more time to nurture myself back to wholeness. I needed to embody my authentic self before I could truly be of service to others.

To my ego, turning down such a rare opportunity to work with Lisa was crazy. To my soul, it was the only choice.

Once you begin living from your soul instead of your personality (ego), the whole of the Universe acts in your favor. So, there is no need to fear you are missing out, or missing opportunities. Life will magically unfold, and things will work out better than you could ever imagine.

The one chapter I submitted at the Maui Writers Conference was published as a chapter in this book. Not only did my book become a best seller, but I also had a chance to personally present Lisa Nichols with a copy during one of her speaking engagements. My intention was simply to express gratitude for her graciousness. To my surprise and delight, she invited me up on stage to congratulate me.

ଓଓଓ

Something for You

Throughout our lives, we are continually growing and expanding because we are continually defining and redefining our desires and intentions. There is no finish line. So, wherever you are in this moment is perfect.

By choosing to explore your beliefs about yourself instead of deferring to your ego's reaction to the world, you'll begin to consciously view yourself more objectively, honestly, and compassionately.

We must love ourselves, respect our uniqueness, and appreciate our gifts. Whenever we look to others for validation of our worthiness, we give away our power.

Self-love is empowerment. And the magic of self-love is, once we no longer need the approval of others, we are free to be our authentic self.

An important step to living as your authentic self is to recognize when your ego is in the driver's seat. How do you know? By being in the present moment and noticing what emotions you are feeling. If they feel bad, your ego is driving on autopilot.

For example, when I was making the video for Lisa Nichols, I felt excitement. Yet, when I watched the video, the excitement turned to anxiety. I realized that if I was rejected, it would reinforce my feeling of unworthiness.

That's why I knew I had to decline Lisa's offer. I didn't want to join her team to validate my worthiness. It was contrary to the very thing she represents, self-empowerment. If I was to be an advocate for others, I first had to be an advocate for myself.

Seeking approval is often so subtle that we may not be consciously aware that we are doing it. For example, when I tell my husband I'm going shopping, it may seem I'm just letting him know my plans. But, perhaps I'm wanting his approval.

Let's be honest. If he said, "Great, honey, have fun and buy yourself something nice," I'd probably faint from shock! More likely, he'll say, "Again?" So, why do I even bother telling him? Because it would be nice to get his approval, his validation that I am worthy of having what I want.

Once I questioned my true motivation for telling him, I realized I was giving my power and enjoyment away by seeking his approval. Now, I just go shopping and enjoy myself.

Below are a few questions for you to consider. Be easy with yourself. We are all in this together. Each of us has a protective personality that is simply trying to keep us safe by keeping us in predictable patterns. It's part of being human. Yet, if you want *something more* for your life, you must get back into the driver's seat and shift gears.

Before you respond to the questions below in your journal, take a few minutes to get out of your head and into your heart. Sit comfortably and relax your neck and shoulders. Relax your jaw, close your eyes, and take several deep belly breaths. Focus on your breath until you feel calm.

- Where in your life do you look for approval from others?
- What would you do differently if you didn't need their approval?
- Visualize yourself at a time in the future when you no longer need anyone's approval. How would that feel?
- What is one small action step you could take to do something you desire without asking for permission or approval?

Just the action of bringing yourself into present moment awareness and witnessing when you are seeking approval will begin to put you back in the driver's seat. All your power is in the present moment.

I am no longer an imitator, a regurgitator, a pretender.
I am the person I came here to be.
I am me.

CHAPTER 10

Believing Is Seeing

Create a vision and never let the environment, other people's beliefs, or the limits of what has been done in the past shape your decisions. Ignore conventional wisdom.

~ Tony Robbins

My heart was pounding in my chest, my palms were sweaty, my breathing was shallow. It was as if I were back in driver's education and taking my first driver's test all over again. Why does that happen every time I drive into a Department of Motor Vehicles parking lot?

The Kendall County DMV was the tiniest of any I've ever seen in the four decades I've been driving. Wedged in between a pizza parlor and nail salon in a small strip center, it wasn't even visible from the street, let alone intimidating.

But, at sixteen years old, I'd flunked my driving test three times in a row because I could not parallel park my parents' gunboat of a car, a 1965 Oldsmobile Delta 88. I'd passed the written test with flying colors and every other aspect of my driving test, except the parallel parking. After the third try, the DPS agent just shrugged his shoulders, rolled his eyes, and signed my permit. To this day, I have never parallel parked.

Usually, I renew my license online. There are no long lines, and I get to keep the same photo on my license for another five years.

I know. Most people hate their driver's license photograph. My husband looks like a wanted criminal in his. But once you hit forty, it's nice to live in denial for as long as possible.

But, this was my first move in twenty years to a new city, and it required an address change. Besides, the ten-year-old photo was making everyone look twice these days.

Before I left the house to drive here, I'd set my intentions for this to be quick and easy, so I was not surprised to find a parking space right in front of the door. I sat in the car with the engine running for a few minutes while I closed my eyes and visualized how I wanted this experience to unfold.

Over breakfast that morning, I mentioned to my husband that I'd love to have the eyeglasses requirement taken off my driver's license.

"That's not possible," he said. "No one ever gets that restriction taken off unless they've had eye surgery."

"Just because it's no one else's reality, doesn't mean it can't be mine," I replied.

"Well, if you can get what you want out of the DMV, you *are* a miracle worker. I'll believe it when I see it," he said.

"You've got it backwards, babe. You've got to believe it before you can see it," I said. "Anything is possible."

The restriction had been placed there over twenty-five years ago. I always hated wearing glasses and read somewhere that wearing them could weaken your eyes and make you dependent on them. That was just the excuse I needed to quit wearing them.

But, once when I got pulled over for speeding five miles over the limit, I was also fined for not wearing my glasses. The fine was more than the speeding ticket.

After that, I always felt like a criminal when I drove without them. I kept them on my car visor just in case I got pulled over again. I used to buy prescription sunglasses, but they were ugly, expensive, and I kept losing them.

So, as I sat in my car, I envisioned myself moving quickly and easily through the process of filling out the change of address forms. I saw myself standing behind the line painted on the floor, having a great picture taken of me smiling and looking younger than ever.

I saw myself walking into the DMV with perfect eyesight. Then I imagined how free I would feel with the eyeglasses requirement removed from my license. How nice it would be to buy regular sunglasses from any designer in any department store. Freedom, ease, fun.

As I entered the DMV, a cowbell attached to the door clanged loudly. As I looked around the room, I was amazed to see three smiling clerks sitting behind their desks along the back wall. There was only one other person in the entire room—a teenage boy taking a written exam.

This was already a day of miracles. Front parking space, no lines, and smiling DMV clerks.

"Hi, I'm Cindy. How can I help you today?" a woman asked as she motioned for me to sit at her desk.

"I just moved here, and I need to change my address and renew my license," I replied.

"Okay. Fill out this form, and then we'll do the eye exam and take a new photo."

I started to get up from my chair to complete the forms at another table.

"No, that's okay," said Cindy. "Sit here and be comfortable. Would you like some coffee?"

I thought, *What planet am I on? Have I died and gone to heaven?* It was like being in the Twilight Zone, only a good version.

"Sure, that would be wonderful. I take mine black."

I finished my paperwork as she returned with my coffee.

"All done?" she asked. I nodded. "Okay, let's do the eye exam. Do you wear glasses or contacts?"

"No, not really," I replied.

Cindy glanced at the back of my old driver's license. "Do you need them?" she asked.

"Not really."

"Well, let's see. Read the bottom line for me," she instructed.

I peered into the machine, which looked like a set of binoculars on steroids, and began reading the bottom line. I only guessed at two of the letters, or perhaps they were numbers.

"That's pretty good, but let's try it again. Maybe we need to tilt this to fit you better since you're so tall," she said.

As she adjusted the machine, I said to myself: *I can see clearly NOW*, and smiled, knowing I would pass.

I took a deep breath, leaned up to the machine and the hazy letters magically transformed. I read them quickly without any error.

Cindy smiled at me and said, "Happy Birthday! You passed. I'm taking this restriction off your license!"

I felt like I'd just won the lottery. As I stepped over to the wall and stood behind the blue line painted on the floor to have my picture taken, I was grinning like a Cheshire cat.

That was so much fun!

Believing IS seeing. Maybe it's time to try parallel parking again.

What the mind can conceive, it can achieve.
~ Napoleon Hill

Two weeks later, Mark walked into the kitchen with the mail. "You've got something here from the Department of Motor Vehicles," he said.

I ripped open the envelope, scanned the front and back of my license, and started dancing around the kitchen. "Woohoo!" I yelled.

"What's that all about?" he asked.

I handed him my driver's license.

"Man, that's a good picture. Why were you smiling so big?"

"Turn it over," I said.

He looked at the back of the license. "What? I don't see anything."

"Exactly! No restrictions. I'm free at last!" I shouted.

Mark grinned and handed me my Chanel sunglasses and my purse. "Where are we going?" I asked.

"To buy a lottery ticket," he replied. "And you're picking the numbers!"

ᘓ ᘓ ᘓ

Something More

You create your reality moment by moment, thought by thought. What you believe to be true in this moment will be your experience. When you think of what you want and don't offer any resistant thoughts, it will manifest quickly because you are in alignment with your desire.

When you are happy with who you are and with what you have, and at the same time eager for more, that is the optimal vibration for attracting your desire. But if you are feeling worry, impatience, doubt, or unworthiness, you are hindering the manifestation of your desires.

Before I headed to the DMV to renew my license, I was excited and happy about our new home. I was eager to begin a new life in a small town that I fell in love with when I visited as a teenager. And, I truly believed it was possible to have the restriction taken off my driver's license.

Even though my husband doubted it was possible, I allowed him to have his belief and kept my focus on my desire. And, although I misread the eye chart the first time, I kept holding the vision and the essence of a restriction-free license. This allowed the Universe/God/Source/All That Is to inspire the clerk to adjust the machine and offer me a second try. And my strong, unwavering belief allowed me to see the letters and numbers clearly, as if through a magnifying glass.

God is always conspiring in our favor. The challenge for us is to have faith in the Divine and allow the magic to happen.

ᘍᘍᘍ

Something for You

Can you remember a time when your day went so smoothly and effortlessly that it felt like magic? That was pure alignment. So, how do you intentionally create that experience so it becomes the norm instead of the exception?

To be in alignment with your desires, you must focus on them with eager anticipation while feeling gratitude and appreciation for what you currently have in your life. If you are pushing against what is, you just continue to attract what is. Your vibration is the attractor. Always.

If I had tried to justify my beliefs or desires to my husband when he argued that the DMV wouldn't remove my eyeglass restriction unless I had surgery, my resistance would not have allowed my desire to manifest.

For you to receive your desires, you must allow others to have their beliefs whether you agree with them or not. This may be one of the most difficult ideas to get your heart and mind around because the ego will always want to jump in and defend its position.

Remember, fear comes from the ego; love comes from the soul. Fear is resistance. Love is allowing. We cannot be in resistance and allowing at the same time.

So, let's return to your gratitude list from chapter 8. Choose one of the items for this next exercise that you can easily find lots of positive aspects to appreciate.

The state of appreciation is the highest vibration and will put you in the receiving mode. The longer you embody this feeling of appreciation, the more magnetic you become to ALL your desires. And the good news is, it doesn't matter what topic you use to raise your vibration.

- Once you have your topic, set your timer for three minutes.
- In your journal, write a letter of gratitude describing all the ways your topic has brought joy or happiness to your life. Try to use the full three minutes. Be creative.
- For example, if I were to pick the topic of lady bugs, I might write: I love lady bugs. They make me smile with their bright-red bodies and black polka dots. I love how they are so gentle and how they tickle my skin as they walk across my hand. I appreciate how much they do for us and the environment. I love that they protect our crops, plants, and flowers from destructive insects. I love watching the smiles on children's faces when they discover a ladybug on the sidewalk or windowsill.

- Once you complete your letter, read it out loud (your unique voice will add another dimension to your attracting ability).
- Notice how your body feels. You can carry this higher vibration intentionally, and when you notice it dipping, just think of your topic and it will rise.

Challenge

Continue to write letters of appreciation for the items on your list whenever you want to raise your vibration. For as you continue to practice, you create new neural pathways which will eventually become your new set point. That's when you become the intentional creator that you came here to be, living in joy and eager for more.

CHAPTER 11

Indian Summer

We turn thoughts into facts, and facts into stories, and we carry these stories around as if they're truth.

~ Jon Kabat-Zinn

"*The Drake* stopped at Alexandria, Bengasi, Tripoli, Tunis, and Algiers, passed the Rock of Gibraltar, and turned north up the coast of Portugal. Now they were off Cape Finisterre on the coast of Spain, and in a few days, Captain Watson told Alec, they would be in England..."

"My dad's from England!" shouted Olivia, as I paused in reading *The Black Stallion* aloud to a group of eleven-year-old girls.

"My grandparents are from Spain," added Adriana.

The Boerne Library's Summer Literacy Camp was underway, and since only girls had chosen to participate, the atmosphere was more like a giant slumber party.

"Can you make an educated guess from this paragraph what country Alec is from?" I asked.

"From England?" Olivia replied.

"What gives you clues that England is his home?" I asked. My niece's hand shot up into the air. "Yes, Chelsea?"

"He's probably from England because it sounds like he's returning home, 'cause in the first chapter he was thinking about his two months in India for the summer with his uncle Ralph in the jungle."

"Yeah," added Olivia. "So, since he's about our age, he has to go home because school is about to start."

"I love how you related your own experience to the story to figure that out, Olivia," I replied. "And you're both correct. He is from England."

"Mrs. Wells, did American Indians come from India?" asked Susie.

"That's a great question, Susie. Does anyone know the answer?"

"I think it has something to do with Christopher Columbus. He thought he was in India or something," answered Laura.

"Oh, yeah, I remember," added Chelsea. "He discovered America when he was looking for a new trade route, but thought he was in the East Indies, so he named the people Indians."

"So, why didn't he rename them when he found out he made a mistake?" asked Susie.

"Probably because he didn't want to look dumb to the Queen," replied Olivia.

"So, we still call them something they're not? That's confusing," said Susie.

"I agree it's a bit confusing," I added. "That's why people from India call themselves East Indian and those here in America are usually called Native Americans or American Indian. And, of course there are different Native American tribes. My grandmother was a Navajo Indian."

"I'm part Cherokee," added my niece, Chelsea.

"I didn't know your Mom was part Cherokee, Chelsea," I replied.

"She's not. Dad's Cherokee," she said.

"Well, that's funny. I believe we're Navajo, and my brother believes we're Cherokee."

"I'm part Cherokee," said Sarah.

"My dad's parents came from India, so I'm American Indian in a different way," teased Anjuli.

"This sounds like a fun topic of conversation for your lunch break. Why don't y'all go ahead and take your break now," I suggested.

As the giggling gaggle of girls grabbed their lunch bags and headed outside to sit under the trees, I dug my cell phone out of my purse to call my mother.

I was curious why my brother thought we were Cherokee. Certainly, we must be Navajo. After all, my grandmother worked for the Bureau of Indian Affairs and lived on a Navajo reservation.

Whenever she came to visit us, she would bring presents of handmade Navajo bracelets, rings, and woven rugs. She even sang Navajo lullabies about dreams and dream catchers.

Just a couple of years ago, my husband and I had taken my mother on vacation to New Mexico. She was excited about visiting the Navajo reservation, and we ended up purchasing several items including jewelry, pottery, blankets, and books about the Navajo culture.

"Hi, Mom, I have a quick question for you about our Indian heritage," I said.

"Hi, Hon. I thought you were teaching today."

"I am, but during a discussion this morning about the difference between East Indians and American Indians, Chelsea shared that she was Cherokee."

"I didn't know her mom was part Cherokee," Mom replied.

"She's not. That's what I wanted to ask you about. Chelsea said her dad told her he was Cherokee right after I mentioned to the class that we were Navajo. Do you know why he might think we're Cherokee?"

"Well, I don't know. And I'm not sure why you believe we're Navajo," she said.

"What do you mean? We're not Navajo?" I asked.

"No, we're Sioux," she said.

"Are you kidding me?"

"No, I'm serious. Why did you think we were Navajo?"

"Because Grandma lived and worked on a Navajo reservation, and everything she bought us was made by Navajos.

She never talked about being Sioux. Neither did you," I said.

Mom laughed. "Even though your grandmother was Sioux, when she worked for the Bureau of Indian Affairs she was assigned to work with the Navajo tribe."

"So why did you buy all that Navajo stuff in New Mexico?" I asked, still not wanting to let go of my story.

"Because they reminded me of my childhood. My mother was always buying things to support the Navajo community, so our house was filled with Navajo textiles, pottery, and baskets."

"Oh my gosh! That's hilarious! I've been telling others I'm Navajo for over forty years. I can't believe we never had a conversation about this. It just shows how easily we can live our whole life based on false beliefs."

The most erroneous stories are those we think we know best—and therefore never scrutinize or question.

~ Stephen Jay Gould

ଓଓଓ

Something More

When Chelsea made the statement that we were Cherokee, I could easily have assumed she was wrong and defended my story. Yet, by being open and curious, I discovered I was carrying a false belief based on a childhood perception.

Everyone is focused on their own story which they create from their unique perspective. And that story is only true for them. Chelsea assumed she was Cherokee because she remembers my sister-in-law telling her that story. And my sister-in-law remembers hearing it from my brother.

I assumed we were Navajo because of the evidence I gathered growing up, and from that evidence I created a story. I lived almost fifty years of my life believing my story and making choices based on something that wasn't true.

None of us was living the truth! We never thought to question our assumptions. We never thought to ask for information or confirmation from my mother. That's because the personality (ego) feels out of control when it is challenged. So, it rigidly defends the identity it has created through our set of beliefs, patterns, and ideas.

One piece of information from my mother and my story changed forever. Once I acknowledged the truth that we were Sioux, my ego immediately began looking for evidence to support my new belief. For example, I remembered a Sioux prayer my grandmother shared with us when we were little. And the fact that the town where she grew up was near a Sioux reservation. Information that I already had but was invisible to my conscious mind because it didn't match my previous belief.

Our belief system is like a mirror that only shows us what we believe. Everything else becomes invisible to us. And, most of our beliefs are based on assumptions. So, when we intentionally change our story, we change our thoughts and our actions. We open to new possibilities and opportunities and our life transforms.

ઉ ઉ ઉ

Something for You

There's *something more* to be aware of when making assumptions. When we assume, we are simply guessing. And we often make a *guessing story* out of our assumptions. And if we share our *guessing story* with others, they will either agree and add their assumptions or disagree causing us to defend our story. Either way, it now becomes a belief.

Making assumptions and taking them personally, causes a lot of unnecessary suffering in our lives. Have you ever had the experience of driving on the freeway and someone zips around you in traffic and cuts you off? What assumptions did you make in that situation?

Perhaps, like me, you might think, "What a jerk. He's so selfish risking someone else's life just to get a few feet ahead in traffic. What if he had hit me? He could have killed me." These thoughts and assumptions then lead to feelings of anger and fear.

The incident lasted a split second. But if I called my friend and my sister and my husband to repeat my *guessing story* to validate my viewpoint, I would continue to experience fear and anger for hours and maybe even days. All because I made assumptions and took them personally.

What's true is always what's happening in the present moment, not the story about what *should* or *shouldn't* happen. What's true is someone in a car cut in front of me on the freeway and took me by surprise. That's it.

Everything else is a *guessing story* based on assumptions. I don't know if he's a jerk. I don't know if he's selfish. I don't know why he cut in front of me. He didn't hit me. He didn't cause an accident. I don't even know if the driver is a "he." I'm making it all up in my imagination.

If I simply observed what happened and chose to be grateful that I was safe, I would have no need for a story. And I'd default back to my natural state of well-being, which puts me in vibrational alignment with all the things I desire.

We are the creators of our reality. If we want more joy and happiness in our life, we must be willing to observe the stories we tell and honestly acknowledge when we are filling in the gaps with assumptions.

- Choose one conversation this week and consciously pay attention to the stories you share.
- In your journal:
  - Write the story and give it a title.
  - At the end of the story, write down the emotions and feelings that came up as you wrote the story.
  - Next, read the story and put parenthesis around any assumptions you made.
  - Now, reread the story ALOUD leaving out the assumptions.
  - Notice if the feelings that came up for you are different without the assumptions.

Now that you are aware your personality will always want to fill in the gaps of your stories with assumptions, you can consciously choose to tell better feeling stories.

CHAPTER 12

Up, Up, and Away

Most of us have never allowed ourselves to want what we truly want, because we can't see how it's going to manifest.
~ Jack Canfield, quoted in *The Secret*

W hat's that frown for?" my husband asked as he stood in the doorway of my home office.

"I'm thinking that traveling could be a lot easier than this! To get from Corpus Christi, Texas, to Vancouver will take twelve hours of flying with all the plane changes and layovers."

"It's the security lines, customs, and the layovers that drive me crazy," he replied.

"I was looking at an American Express travel magazine and saw an ad for a private jet company. Wouldn't that be great!" I said.

Mark's eyes got big, like a deer in headlights. "You're not serious, are you? How much does that cost?"

"It would run about $150,000 or more."

"You mean you already checked? No way, you're crazy! That's the price of a house."

"Well, if it's true that we create our own reality, and that we can be, do, and have anything we want, I want a private jet ride!"

"Where will you get the money?" Mark asked.

"I don't have to figure that out. My job is to get into the feeling of having it and believe that Source is working on it. To have fun with the idea of it and allow the Universe to surprise me!"

"Good luck with that," Mark replied. "Meanwhile, you better finish making our travel and flight arrangements."

As he walked away, I took a break from my computer to browse through my travel magazine. We had talked and dreamed many times over the years about traveling to Alaska, and now our dream of cruising the Inside Passage was just weeks away. Our friends, Richard and Rebecca, were joining us, and we had already reserved our excursions for the trip.

As I flipped through the pages of my American Express magazine, I came across the advertisement for a private jet service. What *would* it be like to fly in a private jet?

My mind drifted back to a time in my twenties when the man I was dating surprised me by showing up at my office to take me to dinner. "So where are we going?" I asked.

"It's a surprise," Roy said. "But I can guarantee, you've never been to this restaurant before."

As we drove along Loop 410 in northeast San Antonio, I began singing along with an old song playing on the radio about leaving on a jet plane.

Roy laughed.

"I know my singing voice is terrible, but I like this song," I said.

He just smiled and pointed to the freeway sign: San Antonio Airport.

"That's a fun coincidence," I said.

"Well, not really."

Before I could figure out what he was talking about, he drove into a private hangar and parked the car.

"What are we doing here?" I asked.

"Let's go inside. I need to make some flight arrangements."

"For what?" I asked.

"For the best steak dinner in Texas!"

An hour later we were in his private Cessna airplane headed for a little Texas ranch town in the middle of nowhere.

I had never been in a private airplane before. I was surprised how easily the plane lifted into the air. It felt like I was free-floating in the clouds as we watched the sun dip below the horizon.

About thirty minutes later, we approached a landing strip used by crop-dusting planes, and we needed every inch of it to land. When we stepped out of the plane, a black sedan was waiting to take us to the restaurant.

"It looks closed," I said, as we drove into the parking lot.

"It is. They closed at nine o'clock."

Roy was a personal friend of the owner, who had prepared a meal especially for us. We were the only diners in the restaurant, and it was the best steak I've ever eaten.

*Imagination is everything. It is the preview of life's
coming attractions.*

~ Albert Einstein

As I continued thinking back to that night—the delicious food, the friendly restaurant owner, the surprise and delight of my first private airplane ride, the sparkling lights in the dark of night as we landed in San Antonio—I felt the same joy and fun and freedom as if I were reliving the experience.

And then I began imagining what it might feel like to experience a private jet ride, bigger and faster and farther. Wouldn't it be fun to drive to a private hangar and park a few feet from the plane? To have private pilots to load our luggage, whatever weight we wanted to pack! Wouldn't it be nice to sit in a lounge a few hundred feet from the plane, drinking coffee and relaxing in leather lounge chairs while the pilots cleared us for takeoff?

Wouldn't it be amazing to simply climb the stairs to our luxurious seats, no security line, no fumbling with shoes, no crowds or long lines, no customs—just ease and comfort?

Wouldn't it be fun to stand up and walk around on the plane, change seats, play real cards on a real table, fix our own drinks, and eat delicious food using real tableware?

And wouldn't it be fantastic to fly nonstop direct from Corpus Christi, Texas, to Vancouver in a matter of a few hours?

I was getting excited. I could picture it all. I could feel the freedom and fun of it.

I tore the picture of the jet from the magazine and tossed it into my magical creation box along with my other dreams. As I closed the lid, I read aloud the phrase I had painted on the top, "And so it is!"

The next day, as I was working in my office, the phone rang. "Hey, Richard. I was just sending you an email with our travel confirmations. Our seats are right behind yours on the first flight," I said.

"Well, we may have a slight change of plans. I'm calling to ask you a big favor. And we want you to know that it's okay to say no if it doesn't feel comfortable," he said.

"What's up?" I asked.

"A close friend of ours passed away about a month ago, and his wife, Margaret, is having a hard time working through her grief. We thought a trip might help her, and we're wondering how you guys felt about inviting her to join us on the cruise."

I hesitated before answering.

"I'll take care of making all the travel arrangements for her," he quickly added. "I'm not even sure she'll accept the invitation."

My clear intention and expectation for fun on this trip was so solid that nothing could deter my enthusiasm. "No problem, Richard. Go ahead and invite her. It might be the change she needs to lift her spirits."

"Thank you so much, Kat. I know just being invited will help her feel better. I'll get back to you."

You don't need to know how it's going to come about. You don't
need to know how the Universe will rearrange itself.

~ Joe Vitale

Three days later, my cell phone rang. The caller ID showed
it was Richard. Before I answered, I thought, *No matter what, my*
intention is to have a fun trip. Everything always works out for me.

"Hi there, Richard. I'm guessing you're calling about
Margaret."

"First, let me ask you how you feel about canceling our
flight plans?" he asked.

"What! Why?" I asked, completely taken by surprise.

"Margaret has decided to join us on the cruise. But her
only request is that we allow her to fly us to Vancouver on her
private jet!" he shouted.

I jumped out of my chair and danced my happy dance
around my desk. "Are you joking? Are you serious? Oh, my
gosh! Wait until I tell Mark!"

"Tell me what?" Mark asked, as he stepped into my office
shaking his head at my antics.

"I'll call you back, Richard. Let me tell Mark the good news!"

"What's going on?" Mark asked.

"We are flying on a private jet directly from here to Vancouver
and back!" I yelled.

"What? What did you do? How?" he asked.

Excitedly, I related my conversation with Richard. "She
doesn't like flying commercial, and since her pet sitter is here in

Corpus Christi, she's flying down from Santa Fe, New Mexico, to drop off her dog and to pick the four of us up! Can you believe it?"

The disbelief on Mark's face was priceless. "Are we really flying on a private jet? Is this a joke? How is that possible? You just made that statement a few days ago. How can you get something so big so fast?"

"Because, since I had no clue of how or where or when it would manifest, I *had* to leave it to the Universe. Plus, I had no resistance because I had never considered it before the other day. I just found a way to feel what flying in a private jet feels like as if I had already experienced it and then allowed the Universe to do its magic."

You can start with nothing, and out of nothing and out
of no way, a way will be made.
~ Michael Bernard Beckwith

೮೮೮

Something More

Creation starts with a desire and your imagination. The more you can feel the essence of your desire and incorporate all your senses into envisioning it, the more real it will feel to you. The more real it feels, the stronger your belief becomes that it will manifest. What you believe you receive.

Desire + Imagine + Believe + Surrender = Creation.

Desire: Your desire for something more in your life is your asking.

Imagine: Using your imagination is your magnetic point of attraction.

Believe: Your belief is strengthened by acting as if your desire has manifested.

Surrender: Surrendering the need to control how your desire manifests will allow the Universe to surprise and delight you.

DIBS: When you call dibs on something, you claim it in advance and you expect to receive it. Calling DIBS is deliberate creation in action. I used DIBS to claim my private jet ride, and I use it with my clients to guide them through the creation process.

One of my clients, let's call her Sophia, needed guidance for an upcoming opera audition. Although she had performed in many operas, this one had a higher level of difficulty. She was eager to get any part, just for the opportunity to improve her craft.

Sophia explained that each time she envisioned herself on stage, she would become so anxious that she considered backing out of the audition. I explained to her that it was simply her ego trying to protect her from disappointment in case she didn't get a part in the opera. And that if she was willing to use her imagination to role-play, she could shift that anxious feeling to one of excitement.

She agreed to play along. She took the role of an opera singer giving an interview after a stellar performance. My role would be as a journalist for a high-end publication. During the interview, I asked questions that activated all her senses: sight, sound, taste, touch, and smell. What was she wearing? What color was her costume? How did the fabric feel on her body?

I asked her to describe her dressing room and the green room, the sights, smells, sounds, tastes. I asked her how it felt to be on stage performing with such talented actors. I had her describe the audience giving her a standing ovation and the emotions she was feeling.

Once we completed the interview, Sophia was in tears. She was already living the essence of her desire, joy, and passion through her imagination. She was excited about her audition and no longer attached to the outcome.

A couple weeks after our session, Sophia called me to let me know that for the first time in her career, she had fun at her audition. And, not only was she invited to join the production, but she was offered one of the leading roles.

Acting as if you have already received your desire, strengthens your belief and magnetizes the thoughts, people, circumstances, and events to bring it about.

Sophia's desire to be in the production and her willingness to use her imagination increased her belief that it was possible.

She maintained her alignment with her desire because she surrendered the need to control the outcome. She was already living in the essence of her desire, so she had no resistance. And the Universe/God/Source/All That Is delivered her something even better than she imagined.

🐬🐬🐬

Something for You

Your imagination is the most powerful resource you have for creating a life you love. Everything that exists was first an idea in the imagination of someone who believed in possibilities. The chair you are sitting on was once an idea that someone created using their imagination. The building that you live in was once an idea that someone designed using their imagination. My private jet ride was once an idea that I manifested by using my imagination.

We are the creators living in our own creation. Often, we are subconsciously creating by default because we are reacting to the world around us from old patterns and habits. That's why sometimes it seems no matter how hard we try, nothing changes.

Your creative super power comes from your imagination. When you consciously and intentionally activate that super power, your life will begin to change beyond your wildest dreams.

If you'd like to be an intentional creator, you can begin strengthening your imagination muscles by claiming DIBS on a desire. You'll need your journal and about an hour for this activity. Do your best to complete the activity in one sitting to ramp up the momentum of the positive feeling energy, and to focus your full attention on your desire.

DESIRE: What is something that you desire? It could be as simple as a gift of flowers or front row tickets to a concert. Or, perhaps it's a private jet ride or a Corvette. As Abraham-Hicks likes to say, "It's as easy to manifest a castle as a button." However, sometimes the more resistance you have because of your current beliefs, the more practice time you may require to align your energy. But, it doesn't have to take a long time. I manifested the jet ride in three days and a Corvette in two weeks. Anything is possible. You'll see in the next step how I used this method to manifest a Corvette by simply using my imagination.

IMAGINE: To magnetize your desire, you must first be a vibrational match. What is the essence of how you will feel when you receive your desire? For example, both the jet ride and the Corvette provided the feeling/essence of freedom and fun for me.

Once you are clear on the essence, think of another time when you have felt this way. For me, when I was desiring a Corvette, I remembered the essence of freedom and fun I experienced on the private jet ride. Just remembering that event aligned me with the essence immediately. Stay with your memory until you feel the emotional response in your body. Then imagine yourself already living your desire. I imagined myself driving my new Corvette through the Texas Hill Country. Make it fun!

To embody the essence of your desire even more, take small actions that you would take if you trusted your desire was on its way. For example, before my Corvette showed up in my garage, I did research on Corvettes and decided which accessories and colors were my favorites. I called my insurance company to get a quote for the insurance policy. I also went to a dealership and test drove different models.

Each of these actions helped me to take ownership of my desire. It made receiving the car seem like the next logical step, even though I had no idea of how, when, or where it would manifest. I didn't even share my desire with my husband or anyone else because I wanted to stay in the knowing that my desire was already answered.

BELIEVE: Your belief is strengthened by acting as if your desire has already manifested. This next activity will bridge the gap between IMAGINATION and BELIEF even more. Imagine that you have already received your desire and write a thank you letter to the Universe/God/Source/All That Is for how easily and effortlessly it unfolded. Be as descriptive as possible, incorporating as many of your five senses as possible.

My letter might begin like this: "Dear Universe, I'm so happy and delighted to be driving my new Corvette. I love the speed and responsiveness of this beautiful car. Driving the winding roads through the Texas Hill Country with the top down feels exciting and exhilarating. With the wind in my hair and the warm sun on my face and shoulders, I feel free and on top of the world. I love the smell of new leather seats and the sounds of the powerful engine…"

Continue writing your thank you letter for as long as possible to maintain the feeling of the essence of your desire. Include as much detail as you like, if it feels good to do so. If any detail makes you feel doubt, keep your details more general. Next, read the thank you letter out loud. Adding your unique voice and thanking in advance lets God know that you are ready to receive.

SURRENDER: Sometimes, letting go of the how, who, where, and when is the hardest part of creation. Most of us carry beliefs that we must work hard and put massive effort into achieving our desires. And, as long as we believe it, that will be our experience.

When we try to control how our desire will show up, who will be involved, where and when it will happen, we have tied the hands of the Universe by not allowing other options. And this slows down our manifestations which reinforces our belief that getting what we want is hard.

But, what if it's much easier than we've been taught to believe? What if the Universe knows the perfect timing and has all the resources to answer our request that are outside of our ability to conceive?

The only thing I did to manifest my private jet ride and my Corvette was use my imagination and surrender the how.

The Universe surprised and delighted me in ways I could not have imagined.

My private jet ride came from a stranger. My Corvette was a surprise birthday present from my husband. Without even knowing that I had been dreaming about a new car, my husband wanted to give me a big present for my fiftieth birthday. So, he bought the car and parked it in the garage. But, because I had been so busy unpacking from our recent move, I hadn't left the house. So, the Corvette sat in my garage for two days wrapped in a huge red bow before I even knew it was there.

The car was everything I had imagined, even the color. Best of all, I got my present a year early! I wasn't turning fifty. I was only forty-nine! Thank you, Universe!

CHAPTER 13

Aura You My Friend?

Our spirituality is a oneness and an interconnectedness with all
that lives and breathes, even with all that does not live or breathe.

~ Mudrooroo

A black fly flew up my nose.

"That's disgusting," Martha said, as I blew it out.

Her entire head was covered by the two-dollar hat with netting she had purchased in the gift shop.

"Why aren't you wearing your hat?" she asked.

"The netting's so dark, and I want to enjoy the view of Ayers Rock. I may never have the chance to see it again," I replied. "Besides, the flies aren't that bad."

Martha sighed and shook her head at me as we continued our hike into the caves to take pictures of the hieroglyphics painted on the walls.

Uluru, as the Aborigines call Ayers Rock, is an amazing sight, especially on the day that we arrived. Greenery had sprung up all around its base. The month before our arrival, the usually arid Ayers Rock experienced nearly half a year's rainfall in just one day. In fact, all of Alice Springs was in bloom.

"I can't... akkk!" I spat out a fly that flew into my mouth.

My husband, Mark, laughed at me. Then a black fly flew into his ear. They were a little annoying, but at least there weren't hundreds swarming around us, as we'd been warned could happen.

"They look for moisture," the guide told us. "That's why they swarm around your head."

"I guess that's why the flies aren't so bad today," I said, waving my hands back and forth in front of my face to avoid further fly inhalation. "There are still pools of water everywhere."

"Yes, so take a lot of photographs because you probably won't see Uluru dressed in green again for another fifty years," he replied.

After taking pictures in the caves and all around Ayers Rock, our tour group boarded the buses and headed for the Uluru-Kata-Tjuta National Park Cultural Center.

"I'm starving. I wonder what we're having for lunch?" I said to Martha as we exited the bus.

"I don't know, but I hope they have screens on their windows, or we'll have to eat with our fork in one hand and a fly swatter in the other," she said.

As we entered the dining hall, another tour group was exiting. "We ate it all," one of the tourists said as he held the door for us. And he wasn't kidding. The buffet was nearly empty.

A young brunette dressed in khaki shorts and a matching

shirt with a park ranger patch sewn above the breast pocket whistled loudly above the noise of the grumblings of our group. "We are cooking your food now," she shouted with an Australian accent. "We had an extra tour group this morning we weren't expecting. We apologize for the delay. If you'll take a seat, we'll get your drink orders started. It will be about ten minutes."

I headed to a table near the only window in the room and opened it to let the fresh air in. There was a strong body odor that filled the dining hall, and it was a bit overwhelming. "Martha, do you smell anything?" I asked. "Or is it just me?"

"Yes, it's that Aborigine man dressed in a park ranger uniform standing across the room. The one who's staring at you."

"Wow, the odor is overwhelming to me. I guess the other park rangers and personnel are used to it," I replied.

"I read in my travel book that in their culture, they only bathe when it rains," Martha said.

The Aborigine man was still staring at me when the kitchen staff brought out steaming pots of food to replenish the buffet tables. As tourists from our group rushed the table, I said to Mark, "I think I'll wait until the line goes down a bit."

"Okay, do you want me to bring you anything?" he asked.

"No, thanks, I'll wait."

The Aborigine man was standing at the end of the food line, still staring in my direction. I felt uncomfortable because I didn't know why he was so focused on me. What must he think of all of us, of the thousands of tourists coming from around the world every year to the Aboriginal sacred grounds? It must be like having guests at your home who never leave.

I sat at our table near the open window until almost everyone had been served. The Aborigine continued to lean against the wall at the end of the buffet table. He was a big man, about six foot two inches tall, and appeared to be around thirty years old.

"Are you going to eat?" Mark asked. "Everyone's almost finished."

I took a deep breath of fresh air and got into the buffet line. Immediately, the Aborigine got in line behind me and stood so close I could feel his breath on my hair. What was he doing? *Maybe they don't recognize personal space*, I thought.

I kept trying to move a few more inches forward, but he stayed right up next to me. The smell was so strong that my gag reflex started to kick in. I grabbed a napkin from the table and pretended to cough and held it to my nose so I could catch a breath.

I rushed through the food line as quickly as I could, and when I reached our table, I turned my head toward the open window and sucked in huge gulps of fresh air. This was one of those times when my keen sense of smell was working against me. When I turned back around, I noticed the Aborigine had finally gotten his food and was sitting at a table by himself across the room.

So, what was that all about, I wondered, as I ate my lunch. He didn't look toward me again. He didn't look up at anyone. He simply focused on his food.

I barely finished my meal when the woman park ranger shouted, "Welcome, everyone. My name is Sienna, and I will be your guide and interpreter for the rest of the tour. We ask that you refrain from taking any pictures during the demonstration today. Many Aborigines do not allow their photograph to be taken, and some believe that it steals their soul. Thank you for understanding."

As she guided us outside, I noticed an Aborigine woman was sitting cross-legged on the ground, stoking the campfire in front of her with a large stick. She was barefoot and wore a simple shirt and long skirt.

"Please find a seat," Sienna said to our group of forty people.

I chose to sit on a log where the campfire smoke was drifting so that it would mask the strong body odor of the Aborigine. Others sat on boulders in a semicircle around the fire.

The Aborigine woman began sorting through the stems of dried flowers piled next to her. I was focused on her hands as she expertly stripped the leaves from the stems and used a rock to smash the dried flowers.

When I looked up at her eyes, she was staring straight at me. As she continued to work sifting through the dried powder to remove any stems, her gaze would shift from her work and then back to me.

"The flowers are crushed into a powder and heated over the flame of the fire to make a glue-like substance," Sienna explained.

The Aborigine woman spit on the end of a thick, wooden stick and rolled it in the dried flowers. Next, she held the flower-covered end of the stick over the fire. She repeated this process several times and then attached a rock that had been sharpened into a small axe-like blade to the end of the stick.

When she finished, she passed it around for us to look at it. As I held it in my hand, I was amazed how strong and sturdy it was. I glanced in her direction, and she was staring at me.

I smiled and said, "Beautiful," and she nodded her acceptance of my compliment.

"Amazing," I said to Mark. "Can you believe she made this from a rock, a stick, some dried flowers, and spit!"

"And the glue is made from flowers and spit. Crazy!" he replied.

The more you know, the less you need.
~ Australian Aboriginal saying

Sienna held up a doughnut-shaped item that looked like it was made from fabric, and said, "Next, she will demonstrate how to make this object from the stems left over from making the glue. We won't tell you what it's used for, yet. It's a surprise."

The Aborigine swiftly sorted the stems into piles and began weaving them together to form a circle. Every few seconds, she would pull out a strand of hair from her head and add it to her weaving. Her hands moved swiftly, yet she never looked at what she was doing. Instead, she was looking at me. When our eyes met, she pointed at her head.

Even Sienna, who was explaining the process to us, looked to see what the Aborigine was staring at. When she saw it was me, she just smiled.

"Hey, Kathy," someone in the group yelled out. "I think she wants some of your blond hair for her doughnut."

There were at least twelve other blonds in the group. *Why me?* I thought.

When the woman completed the doughnut, she placed it on top of her head, stood, and placed a large ceramic pot on top of the doughnut. It balanced perfectly.

Sienna explained, "The Aborigine women use the doughnuts to balance water jugs and other items on their heads so they can keep their hands free."

The audience applauded, and the Aborigine woman walked away. As the tour group scattered and headed toward the gift shops and museum, I walked up to the park ranger and told her about my experience in the dining hall. I asked if she knew why both Aborigines were staring at me so intently.

"The Aborigines live in nature and are in tune with the energy of the earth. One of their gifts is the ability to see auras. They weren't staring at you, they were looking at your aura," she said.

"But, why was the young man standing so close to me in the dining hall?" I asked.

She smiled and said, "I'm glad you weren't offended. I've never seen them do that with a tourist before. It is the highest compliment. He got close to you so that he could stand in the energy of your aura."

We are all visitors to this time, this place. We are just passing through. Our purpose here is to observe, to learn, to grow, to love... and then we return home.

~ Australian Aboriginal saying

ᘒᘒᘒ

Something More

You either believe this world is a safe place or a dangerous place. Whichever perspective you choose can create fear, doubt, and mistrust, or it can generate curiosity, understanding, and love. You get to choose in every moment.

If I had chosen to be offended instead of curious when the Aborigine park ranger stared at me or started telling myself a story that there was something to fear from him, my aura would have dimmed and most likely, he would have turned away. And I would have missed out on the beautiful interaction and powerful affirmation that we are all connected.

Our auras communicate nonverbally with other people. The more vibrant your aura, the more peace and calm others feel in your presence. The human aura is ever changing and is affected by a person's health and well-being.

And, since our physical well-being is determined by our emotional well-being, our thoughts and beliefs affect the radiance of our auric field. The higher our vibration, the larger and brighter our aura. The lower our vibration, the smaller and duller our aura.

The thoughts you think, the words you speak, the stories you tell also vibrate. We've all experienced the need to move away from someone who is putting off a negative vibe. Most likely they were in fear, anger, or judging another. So even without saying a word, you were picking up on their vibration from their auric field.

Our auras also interact directly with the Law of Attraction, magnetizing people, things, and events that are a vibrational match. That's why it's important to live in the present moment and be aware of the stories we tell and the thoughts that we choose to focus on.

Everything is energy, and that's all there is to it. Match the frequency of the reality you want, and you cannot help but get that reality. It can be no other way. This is not philosophy. This is physics.

~ Albert Einstein

The book you are holding in your hand, the chair you are sitting on, the colors you see around you, the sounds you hear are all vibrating energy. Everything is connected to everything else in one big, unified field. That's how you attract the life you are living by the thoughts you think and the beliefs you hold.

Scientific research and techniques such as electrophotography have shown that all matter radiates an electromagnetic field — auric field. My first experience with electrophotography was years ago during a visit to Edgar Cayce's Association for Research and Enlightenment (ARE) where I attended *The Artist's Way* weekend seminar with Julia Cameron.

During intermissions, the ARE offered attendees a free aura photography session. After they completed mine, three of the staff members were whispering as they looked over my results. I had sprained my ankle and was wearing a cast, so I thought perhaps it had affected the outcome of the photos.

When they finally shared the results with me, one of the staff members said, "We have never seen such a large and vibrant aura before. What's even more amazing is that you're injured. Usually injuries will dull the vibrancy of the auric field."

That experience made me curious and was a turning point in my life. It led me to study bioenergetics, specifically energy flow through living systems. So, when the park guide, Sienna, explained the Aborigines were trying to stand in my auric field, I understood why.

ය ය ය

Something for You

We are the initiators of the vibration we send out to the unified field. We have the power to mold and shape energy through our consciousness. But, if we are living our life on autopilot, reacting to our environment, then we create our life based on subconscious belief patterns. That's why things never seem to change no matter how much we want them to.

Creating a life you love requires you to consciously set intentions and choose to focus deliberately. The Universe is always responding to your requests and does not discriminate between wanted and unwanted. It is simply responding to your vibration.

Have you ever been to a grocery store when all the checkout lines were long? Perhaps you rushed up to the shortest line hoping to beat the crowd only to discover your short line was moving slower that the longer lines. Why does this happen?

Even though your intention was to get out of the store quickly (wanted), trying to avoid long lines (unwanted) was the dominant vibration. So, the Law of Attraction responded.

The solution is to focus on the essence of your desire, for example, ease and flow. As you're holding the feeling of ease and flow, the Universe will guide you to the best line. And perhaps it's the longest line, because the Universe knows that someone is on their way to open another register and the clerk will wave you over to their counter.

The Universe and everything in it—including us—may, in fact, be part of a grand cosmic pattern where all portions are evenly shared by every other.
~ David Bohm, founding father of Quantum Physics

Think of yourself as a radio tower sending out signals to the unified field. Your emotional energy dictates what frequency you are on and everything that is a vibrational match will find you. If you've ever had the experience of thinking of someone you haven't heard from in a long time and suddenly the phone rings and they're on the line, you've experienced the unified field in action.

You don't have to understand quantum physics to mold and shape your life any more than you have to understand chemistry to breathe or gravity to walk upright. Simply trust these principles are at work and you have the power to consciously use them in your favor.

So, let's do a fun experiment to remind you that you have the power of the Universe at your command.

- First, set an intention. Perhaps you'd like to have contact with an old friend you haven't heard from in a while. Or maybe you love ladybugs and want the Universe to show you lots of ladybugs.
- Next, embody how it would feel to experience your intention. Close your eyes and imagine it with all five physical senses.
- Throughout the day, send your intention (friend/ladybugs) loving thoughts.
- Surrender the how and allow the Universe to surprise and delight you.

When I set my intention to see rainbows, it was in the middle of a hot Texas summer when all we have are clear blue skies. My thoughts wanted me to believe it wasn't possible, so I consciously decided that it wasn't up to me to figure out the how and chose to be surprised and delighted.

Within a couple hours, rainbows were showing up everywhere. On an email message from a friend on vacation, on the Hawaiian license plate of a car in front of me at a stoplight, on a calendar I received in the mail, on the T-shirt of a little girl at the coffee shop, and finally in the sky on my drive home after a five-minute shower from one lonely cloud.

Be ready to be surprised and delighted!

CHAPTER 14

Shirt out of Luck

Our intention creates our reality.
~ Wayne Dyer, *The Power of Intention*

The parking lot was nearly full as I swung my Jeep into the parking space nearest the door. I always get the best parking spaces. It's not even a surprise to me anymore. It doesn't matter if it's Christmas Eve at the mall or the day before Thanksgiving at the grocery store. My front row slot is always waiting for me. Friends make me drive because they know the perfect parking spot magically appears for me wherever I go.

What they don't realize is that I create the magic. Every morning after meditation and journaling, I fill out my daily calendar to-do list and pre-pave my intentions for the day. There are two sides to my list. On the left are the things I intend to do and on the right side are the things I leave to the Universe.

Today I expect to find some comfortable shirts at Soma to wear on our trip to Florida. Before I step out of my Jeep, I look over my list.

Written on my side:

Soma

Written on the Universe's side:

Ease and flow in traffic

Best parking space

Friendly salesclerks

Comfortable shirts that fit perfectly

Abundance

Ease and flow through traffic: Check.

Best parking space: Check.

Now I intend to have fun conversations with the sales clerks and to find the perfect shirts for my trip.

As I step out of my Jeep and walk toward the mall, I take time to appreciate the sun shining on my face and the birds singing in the trees above me. For a split-second I wonder why I didn't get a parking space under the shade of the trees, but automatically remind myself that things always work out for me.

I smile as I enter Soma, feeling excited about having fun and seeing what the Universe has in store for me.

"Good morning, my name's Maria. Can I help you find something?"

"No, thanks," I said. "I know exactly what I'm looking for."

As I sifted through the racks of clothes, I found six shirts that I liked, three were in my size and three were a size smaller.

"May I try these on, please?"

"Sure," replied the clerk, as she took the shirts from me and led me to the dressing rooms. "Did you realize that you have two different sizes here?"

"Yes, I'm going to try the smaller size since you didn't have my size in three of the tops. You never know how things might work out."

"Well, good luck," she replied.

"Always," I said.

"What?" Maria asked.

"Things always work out for me," I replied as I smiled and closed the dressing room door. It's all I could say. It would be nice if I could tell her that luck has nothing to do with it; it's all about intention and expectation.

I tried on the three larger shirts first and then the three smaller ones.

"How's it going?" asked Maria. "Can I get you something else?"

"They all fit," I replied through the door, "but I prefer loose fitting over form fitting."

"We can order them online for you," she suggested.

I opened the door and handed her the three smaller tops. "Will you order these three for me, please? I'll go ahead and buy the three that fit."

"Sure, I'll look them up in the computer."

I finished dressing and carried my three shirts to the checkout counter, excited that I had found all the tops I needed for my trip in one store.

"I have bad news," said Maria. "Two of the shirts are available online, but not the leopard-print one."

"That's my favorite one," I said. "I love leopard print." I stood there for a moment, allowing the Universe to do its magic and doing my part by maintaining my belief that I can be, do, or have anything I desire.

Another salesclerk behind the counter asked Maria, "Why don't you call another store and see if they have her size in stock?"

"Good idea, Chelsea. They could ship it to us if you don't mind picking it up here at the store," Maria offered.

"Perfect! Let's do that," I said.

While waiting for the other stores to check their stock, I wandered around and spotted another top I wanted to try on. I was in the dressing room when Maria told me, "I'm sorry, but none of the other stores have this shirt in your size. It's no longer available."

"Okay, thanks. I appreciate you taking the time to make all those calls. I'll be out to pay for the other two in a minute."

As I was dressing, I heard the store telephone ring and then Maria and Chelsea laughing. When I came out of the fitting room they were both looking at me with big smiles on their faces.

"I can't believe it," Maria said. "This has never happened before. That was one of the other stores calling me back. Right after I hung up with them, a woman came into their store and returned the leopard print shirt in your size! She said it was too big and exchanged it for a smaller size."

"The salesclerk at the other store freaked out!" added Chelsea. "She said you are extremely lucky!"

"Things always work out for me," I replied.

"Oh, my gosh!" yelled Maria. "You're not kidding. I just pulled up your account, and you've earned a forty-five percent discount coupon off your total purchase! This is crazy!"

"It just keeps getting better and better," I said.

"Can we be your friends?" asked Chelsea. And we all started laughing.

As I carried my purchases out to my Jeep, I was still smiling at the fun of it all when I happened to notice the two cars parked under the shade of the trees. They were covered, like frosting on a cake, from front to back in white bird poop. All those lovely birds I heard earlier had been taking a restroom break.

Friendly salesclerks: Check.

Comfortable shirts that fit perfectly: Check.

Abundance: Check.

Best parking place EVER! Check.

Things do always work out for me!

Nothing is more exhilarating than to dance through life recognizing that the Universe is there to yield to you whatever you want whenever you want it.

~ Esther and Jerry Hicks-Abraham

CCC

Something More

When you believe things are always working out for you, even when it seems you aren't getting exactly what you asked for, you're able to maintain your good feeling vibration, and the Universe will deliver something even better.

Has there been a time in your life when you wanted something and received even more than you asked for? How did you feel when it happened? Did you think it was luck? Coincidence?

You are the creator of your life, which is a reflection of your energy. Luck has nothing to do with it. That's really good news! Those fabulous experiences were all your creation, and you have the power to create a life you love once you understand that nothing is random.

Things appear and events happen because we are continuously sending out signals to the Universe with our thoughts, words, and focus. Our emotions are like a guidance system letting us know in each moment what type of signal we're sending. If we're feeling good, we're in alignment with our desire; if we're feeling bad, we aren't.

For example, when I was thinking about the tops that I wanted to buy for my trip, I embodied the essence of comfort and beauty before I went shopping. I wore comfortable clothes and shoes to make changing clothes in the dressing room easier. And in the parking lot I focused on the warmth of the sun on my skin and the birds singing in the trees.

And once I found the leopard print top in the store, I set my intention to receive one in my size without being attached to it. This might be a difficult concept to understand at first. I know it was for me in the beginning. How can you want something and at the same time be unattached?

Even though I really wanted that top, and even though I knew without a doubt that the Universe could deliver it, I also had to be okay if it didn't show up. What I usually say to myself to soften my attachment is, "This or something better." Why? Because the Universe/God knows ALL the options available to us and knows ALL our desires.

That's why when we remain unattached and trust that things are always working out for us, we sometimes receive more than we ask for. I didn't know there was an unadvertised, one-day only, in-store sale, but the Universe did. So, not only did I get the shirt that I wanted, I also got a forty-five percent discount on my entire purchase! It's not luck, it's alignment and allowing.

ᘓᘓᘓ

Something for You

So, what is the secret to manifesting your heart's desires? Don't worry, be happy! When we worry, we are not trusting that things are working in our favor. When we worry, we are not living in the present moment. When we worry, we are pre-paving our future with things we do not want. Where thoughts go, energy flows. We are sending a vibrational *worry* signal out into the Universe and the Universe must respond.

Whatever signal you are sending out will magnetize things that match your vibration. Just like when you tune to a radio station, if you set your dial to 101.5 FM you will only receive the music playing on that station. So, if 101.5 FM is your happy station, you will magnetize things that will make you happy.

The good news is you are the one who's in charge of the tuner. You set the tuner with your thoughts and focus. Remember, we have over 60,000 thoughts a day. That's a lot of stations to choose from. Whatever thoughts you choose to focus on will determine what signal you send out into the Universe. So, pick the good ones.

If you'd like to set your tuner more intentionally, it's helpful to set clear daily intentions. When you have clarity, it's much easier to stay focused in the present moment. For many years, I used to-do lists to manage and prioritize all the things I needed to accomplish in a day. The only problem was my list was never ending.

Each time I'd cross something off as completed, I'd usually have two or more items to add to my list. I felt I was getting nowhere, like a hamster on a hamster wheel. Instead of celebrating all that I'd accomplished, I'd beat myself up for not doing more. It certainly wasn't fun!

Even though my to do list was still useful as an ongoing list, I decided I needed *something more* for my daily list. So, I created a daily Ta-Da list.

Ta-da: *an exclamation used as mock fanfare to call attention to something remarkable.*

A Ta-Da list is a short list of only one, two, or three items from your ongoing to-do list that you set as high priority and intend to complete each day. It's important to keep the list short to help you stay focused and feel confident that you will complete your tasks.

For my list, I use a small five-by-six-inch memo pad and draw a line vertically down the middle of the page. At the top of the page I write the day and date. On the left side of the vertical line, I list the one, two or three items I intend to complete for the day. On the right side, I list all the things I want the Universe to handle.

For example, when I went shopping for my tops at Soma, on the left side of my Ta-Da list I wrote only: Soma. I didn't add anything else because I knew shopping would take up most of my day. And if I happened to finish early, I could always choose to do something else from my ongoing to-do list.

On the Universe's side of my Ta-Da list, I wrote: ease and flow in traffic, best parking space, friendly salesclerks, comfortable shirts that fit perfectly, abundance. Notice that I listed things I can't act upon except to set the intention by embodying the essence of my desires: ease, flow, comfort, friendliness, abundance. In other words, just feel good to let it in and the Universe will handle the details.

Once I finish the two sides of the Ta-Da list, at the bottom of the page I write, "This or something better!" This helps me let go of my attachment and allows space for something even better than I could imagine.

If you're like me, your life is busy. And, you're going to do a lot more than just one, two or three things in a day. Perhaps you dropped by the grocery store to pick up a few things, or you stopped to talk to a neighbor who needed your help. Maybe you washed a few loads of laundry, washed dishes, cooked supper, helped your kids with their homework.

You get to take credit for it ALL! The main purpose of the short Ta-Da list is to help you focus and set specific intentions. And it's also to celebrate you! So, at the end of the day, cross through all the items on your Ta-Da list that you accomplished, and on the back of the paper, list all the other things you accomplished throughout the day. NO MATTER HOW SMALL they may seem to you, they matter! Yes, taking your dog for a walk matters. Do your best to write small and fill up the entire backside of the paper.

And once you've finished, take a deep breath and say out loud, "Ta-da!" You are remarkable! By the way, it's almost impossible to shout, "Ta-da!" without raising your hands in the air.

Directions for your Ta-Da list

- Use a small notepad, about five-by-six inches.
- Draw a vertical line down the center of the page.
- Write the day and date at the top of the page.
- List one, two, or three intentions on the left side.
- List everything you want the Universe/God to handle on the right side.

- Write, "This or something better!" at the bottom of the page.
- At the end of the day, draw through or check off the items you completed.
- On the back of the paper, list *everything* else you accomplished throughout the day. Yes, taking a shower counts!
- Celebrate you! Raise your hands and shout, "Ta-Da!"

A little *something more*: It's fun to save Ta-Da lists in a small container for a month or more and reread how much you've accomplished in such a short time.

How do you create miracles in your life?
By understanding that YOU are the miracle maker.
You are of the Divine, living a human experience.
Everything you need to create a miraculous life is within you now.
Be Curious.
Be Courageous.
Be a Conscious Creator.
~ Kat Wells

CHAPTER 15

Heads or Tails

Your imagination is your preview of life's coming attractions.
~ Albert Einstein

The snake's fangs and wide-open mouth got my attention. And then I noticed the woman whose head it was sitting on. It was the most unusual hat at the Women's Shelter Fundraiser: a black-leather top hat with a snakeskin band with the snake's head as the centerpiece. The woman was elegant and striking in her long, black riding jacket, blue jeans, and cowboy boots.

My friend, Linda, introduced me. "Kat, this is Cindy. She's the gala director."

As I greeted Cindy, I heard words come from my mouth that weren't mine. "Hi, Sandy, nice to meet you."

Cindy stared at me with a puzzled look on her face.

"I'm sorry, Cindy. I don't know why I called you Sandy. It just slipped out."

She looked directly into my eyes for a moment and replied, "My dad recently passed away, and his name was Sandy. This was his hat."

All I could think to say was what I knew. "Well, he's here with you, enjoying his hat."

As others walked up to introduce themselves to Cindy, I walked over to the sign-in table with Linda to pick up my bidder's paddle for the auction. I smiled as I thought, *Either Cindy's excited to know that I picked up on the vibration of her dad, or she won't come near me again.*

The theme of the gala was Hats Off. Since we were at the Don Strange Ranch in the Texas Hill Country, many of the hundreds of people were wearing cowboy hats, me included, and the obligatory blue jeans and cowboy boots. Others were a bit more creative. There were Green Bay Packers fans representing the Cheeseheads, dressed head to toe in orange and wearing hats that looked like giant wedges of cheese.

One woman was dressed like a 1920s flapper with a newsboy cap complete with feathers. Others dressed as if they came straight off the television shows *Little House on the Prairie* or *Green Acres*.

As I entered the huge barn where the gala was being held and walked over to the tables where the silent auction items were displayed, someone called out, "Hey, Kat! What are you doing here?"

I turned to see one of my new coaching clients, her arms loaded with Mardi Gras beads.

"Oh, my gosh. I wasn't expecting to see you here, Mary," I said. "What are the beads for?"

"I volunteered to help by selling these for the Heads or Tails game. Do you want to buy some? There's a great prize for the winner, and the beads are only twenty dollars per strand."

"Okay, I'll buy one."

"Are you sure you want only one? You can't win with one. We're selling hundreds of these," she said.

"You know how I've mentioned that all you have to do is set an intention and expect it to happen without any resistance and the Law of Attraction will bring it to you?"

"Yes, but you still need more beads," she said.

From behind me I heard, "No she doesn't. You don't know Kat."

I turned around to see Becca, another of my clients.

"She is a manifesting maniac! If she says she's going to win, she's going to win."

"I am going to win," I said.

Becca turned to Mary and said, "She will win. Just watch!"

As I walked off to meet my husband at our group's dinner table, I thought, Won't it be fun to win the game with both of my clients watching! What a great way to show the Law of Attraction in action.

When I reached our table for ten, my friends were all teasing me because I had only one Mardi Gras necklace for the game. I told them, "I only need one to win."

My husband's friend Bob laughed as he held out his arm loaded with beads. "You can't win with one necklace, Kat."

"She probably will win," my husband said. "But, I think we need to make a bigger donation. Let's go get a few more."

Even though Mark has seen me manifest all kinds of amazing things, he still has some doubt of the power of imagination and expectation. So, we bought a set of six strands for one hundred dollars, and as we walked back toward our table I saw Cindy waving at me. "You're going to win, aren't you," she said.

I answered, "Yes, I am."

She said, "No, really, you are going to win."

And I replied, "Yes, I know."

W-e-e-e! TAP, TAP, TAP. The master of ceremonies was testing his microphone. "Okay, ladies and gentlemen," he said. "Let's get everyone down here on the dance floor for our game of Heads or Tails."

Sixty or more people flooded onto the dance floor. Many had over twenty strands of beads. Several people looked at me holding my seven strands and smiled the smile that says, "You don't have a chance."

W-e-e-e! TAP, TAP, TAP. "Can I have your attention?"

As the master of ceremonies tried to quiet the rumble of the excited crowd, I stood quietly on the dance floor setting my intention to win and enjoying the idea of the reaction that would occur when I won.

"The object of the game is to be the last person standing," said the emcee. "Before I toss this coin in the air, you will put your hand on either your head or on your tail. Then I'll toss the coin. If you have your hand on your head and it lands heads up, you win; but if you have your hand on your tail you lose, and you forfeit a strand of beads. You stay in the game as long as you still have a strand of beads. We have people around the dance floor working as monitors who will collect your beads. Are you ready?"

"YES!" roared the crowd.

"Okay, let's get started. Heads or tails?"

I put my hand on my head and watched the emcee flip the coin in the air.

"Heads!" he yelled.

Several people handed over beads to the monitors.

"Heads or tails?" asked the emcee.

I put my hand on my tail and watch as he flipped the coin, dropped it, and then followed it as it rolled on the floor.

"Tails," he yelled over the noise of the crowd.

After several rounds, I still had all my beads, and half of the original players were out of the game. Then I made the mistake of analyzing the odds of the next flip. Because we had had three heads in a row, logic kicked in and said the next flip had to be tails.

But it wasn't.

As the monitor collected my first strand of beads, I realized that I had gotten into my head instead of trusting my intuition. So, I took a deep breath and quieted my mind.

Several rounds later, I still had six strands of beads, and it was now down to me and one other player. They had us stand back-to-back, like gunslingers of the Old West, so we couldn't see what the other person was doing.

"Heads or tails?" called out the emcee.

I put my hand on my tail. He flipped the coin.

"Tails!" he yelled.

Everyone cheered, but I didn't know if we both got it right or just me. My opponent had about the same number of strands left as I did, so we had five or six more rounds to play depending on whether she lost a strand last round. During the next round, the monitor who was collecting the beads stepped into my line of vision so when I got the next flip correct and everyone was cheering, I could see him step forward and take a set of beads from my opponent.

As I continued to win round after round, the cheers of the crowd got louder and louder. I couldn't hear what anyone was yelling because I was focused on enjoying the excitement and the fun. Finally, I heard the emcee yell, "We have a winner!"

Cindy walked up to hand me the prize, a two-night stay at a downtown hotel on the San Antonio River Walk. She gave me a hug, and said, "I knew you were going to win."

Then I heard someone yell, "You go, Kat!" When I looked up to see who it was, Mary and Becca were jumping up and down, waving their arms.

When I walked back to our table with six strands of beads still on my arm, Bob just shook his head and smiled.

My husband said, "Well, I guess you needed more than one strand after all."

I replied, "Not to win, just to stay in the game."

☾☾☾

Something More

When Mary sold me the Mardi Gras beads, she didn't explain the rules of the game. And I didn't ask. I just wanted to have fun and could already imagine winning. Once I got into the feeling place of it, I knew I was going to win.

Life is like that. We ask. Source answers, "Yes." And our work is to believe.

Did I make a misstep when I didn't ask about the rules of the game? Some might say I would have lost if Mark hadn't bought the extra beads. But, what if I lost one strand because I had the extra beads? We all get to choose how we look at things.

What I know for sure is that calling DIBS on my desire allowed the Universe to provide all the circumstances I needed to win, even though I didn't know the rules of the game.

Desire + Imagine + Believe + Surrender = Creation

I lost one set of beads because I got distracted by the crowd cheering for other people. I lost focus and got into my head trying to analyze probabilities and control the how. Once I surrendered and shifted my focus back to the feeling of fun and excitement, I began to make choices once again from inspiration. And I won!

ᘓᘓᘓ

Something for You

Have you ever given up on a dream because no one believed in you or believed it was possible? Most of us have been influenced by those around us, some well-meaning, some not. And we've been taught to avoid big dreams to prevent disappointment.

The good news is, no matter what others believe, it's your own beliefs and imagination that create the life you're living. And it's through the power of your focus that the Universe is able to support your dreams. The BIG question is: What are you focused on?

Wherever your focus goes, energy flows. Are you focused on the fun and excitement of your dream, or are you focused on all the reasons it won't happen? Are you calling DIBS on your desire, or are you listening to the opinions of others?

Whenever you try something new, it's impossible to have all the answers before you begin. You learn by doing. By taking one small step in the direction of your dream, you set the Universe in motion to support you.

Babies don't learn to walk by taking notes and analyzing all the possible missteps to avoid falling. They start from where they are and take that first step. And once they feel the excitement of movement forward, there's no stopping them.

They don't care if they stumble or fall. They don't care if others laugh at their clumsiness. The possibilities of expanding their world inspires them to keep trying, and with every fall they gather more information, adjust, and finally find their balance.

Like learning to walk takes practice, learning to focus takes practice too. You have over 60,000 thoughts a day, and around ninety-five percent of those thoughts are the same ones you had yesterday. Without learning the skill of focusing intentionally in the present moment, your mind wanders randomly from thought to thought. That's why it feels like your life never changes.

So, how do you build your focus muscle to create the life of your dreams? By practicing with everyday household chores and making it a game. So, let's call DIBS on a household chore. (I bet you didn't see that one coming.)

For example, I used to procrastinate every month for years when it came to balancing my checkbooks and paying bills. I. Dreaded. It! Partly because it took all day long to complete. Partly because it was BORING!

Then, one day I decided to call DIBS on my bookkeeping.

Desire: I was to have fun paying my bills and completing my bookkeeping within four hours.

Imagine: I visualized sitting down at my desk and completing the task effortlessly. I imagined how it would feel to have fun paying bills and balancing my accounts. I asked myself, "What would having fun look like?"

The inspired answer was to time myself and try to beat my time with each checkbook. I also bought an Easy Button from Staples Office Supply. Each time you push the button it says, "That was easy."

Believe: I believed this was going to be fun and that I would finish in record time. I also scheduled lunch with a friend to "act as if" I knew I'd be finished within four hours.

Surrender: Even though my mind kept saying that it was impossible to get a day's work done in four hours and there was no way this would be fun, I surrendered my need to know how it would happen and just trusted the Universe.

Creation: It was so much fun! I set the stopwatch on my iPhone when I started balancing my first checkbook. Once I finished, I wrote down the time it took and was surprised how quickly I had completed it. Then I pushed the Easy Button and laughed...because it was!

I continued with the second checkbook and beat my previous time. With each checkbook, my time improved. When I finished and pressed the Easy Button for the last time, I was laughing.

What had once taken a full day, had taken less than three hours to complete because I stayed focused and was having fun. I realized the reason it used to take so long was my resistance to doing something I found boring and all the interruptions and distractions I allowed to divert my focus.

For several months, I continued setting the timer and improving my time. Now I have fun doing my accounts because I made it a game. Although I no longer time myself, I still use my Easy Button.

Are you ready to give it a try? The key here is to stay focused in the present moment and set the intention to give ALL your attention to the task at hand. Not only will you start strengthening your focusing ability, you'll also experience how the Universe supports you when you have clarity of focus. And, hopefully, you'll find a fun way to do a boring chore.

- Claim DIBS on any household chore that you'd like to experiment with: washing laundry, cleaning dishes, etc.
- In your journal, fill in the information for your DIBS: Desire, Imagination, Belief, Surrender
- During the next month, practice, practice, practice

Remember, it's your focus, your beliefs, and your imagination that create the life you're living. You are a powerful creator!

CHAPTER 16

Will and Grace

Your beliefs about your reality create your experience of it.
~ Orin/Sanaya Roman, *Living with Joy*

Pus was seeping out through the skin on her ankles. Her legs were swollen to three times their normal size. As she sat on the examination table with her pant legs rolled up to her knees, I stood in the doorway, speechless. How could she have let this go so long, and why didn't I notice?

The doctor said, "Your mother needs to go to the hospital right now. She has so much water built up in her body that it has nowhere to go except to burst through her skin."

"I hate going to the hospital," Mom said, as she folded her arms in defiance across her chest.

"Well, Mom, you're in good company. I bet if you took a poll, everyone would agree with you. No one enjoys going to the hospital," I said.

The cardiologist looked a bit shocked at my comment. Being from India, he probably thought I was the rudest daughter he'd ever encountered. And then Mom laughed at my comment, and he looked even more confused.

Mom is strong-willed, big-hearted, and has a wicked sense of humor. And I know the best way to help her deal with fear is with sarcastic banter.

"It's always up to you, Mom. You can go to the hospital or choose to check out. It's your life."

"Well, can I at least go to your brother's restaurant for my last supper before they strap me to all those damn machines?"

The cardiologist fumbled through his papers, obviously uncomfortable with our conversation. "Your mother's heart is not working properly; therefore, the water has been building up for quite some time. Quite frankly, I can't believe she walked in here on her own two feet. I will call the hospital right now and have them set up a room for her."

"How long will it take for them to have the room ready?" I asked.

"About an hour to an hour and a half," he said, as he taped sanitary napkins around Mom's ankles to absorb the water that continued to seep through her skin."

"Good," Mom said. "Then we have time to go to your brother's for lunch."

The doctor gave me a puzzled look, and I just shrugged my shoulders. Obviously, he didn't know that arguing with Mom was a waste of energy.

As she slid off the table and unrolled her pant legs, I realized her baggy pants were camouflaging her swollen legs. No wonder I hadn't noticed.

My mother has never been one to ask for help. Growing up, she had little support from her mother, who worked long hours on the Navajo Indian reservation. Her father was an invalid. She had two brothers, but they were much older and left home when she was very young.

I sometimes wonder if she married my dad at age seventeen because she thought he would take care of her. I don't think she expected that being a military wife would mean being left with four babies to raise on her own. Or that she would be living in a foreign country unable to speak the language and struggling to survive.

"So, what do you want for lunch?" I asked Mom as I helped her into my Jeep.

"I want cheese dip with chips, a bowl of turkey chili, and a glass of wine! They'll just serve me bland crap in the hospital, so I'm going all out," she said, smiling at her own words.

At least this time she didn't fight me about going into the hospital. This would be her fourth trip for congestive heart problems. I used to try and convince her to go, plead with her to listen to the doctors, and use guilt, or whatever it took to get her to concede.

But nothing worked. I just ended up frustrated and angry with her because she didn't seem to care. I was afraid she might die. Usually, it wasn't until she was at death's door and couldn't breathe that she would surrender.

After the last trip to the hospital, when I was sitting with my siblings and in-laws in the intensive care waiting room wondering if she would pull through, I realized that it was my own fear that was creating the struggle. I wasn't minding my own business, I was trying to control Mom's actions so that I felt better. But that wasn't fair to Mom.

When she did pull through, I made the decision that I was going to accept her choices and mind my own business. I would allow her to express her own free will and work on my fears so that I could be in a state of grace with her decisions.

As we headed to the restaurant, Mom said again, "I hate going to hospitals."

"Would you like to feel better about it?" I asked.

"What do you mean?"

"It's all about how we're choosing to look at things. And sometimes our thoughts are on autopilot, and we aren't really aware of how we are focusing," I replied.

"Well, I don't like it because it's depressing. It's bad enough to be hooked up to all those machines and to be eating through a tube. But the worst part is that everyone's so serious, and when I try to joke around with them, they just look at me weird."

"I know, Mom. It's easy to base our expectations on what we've experienced in the past. But what if you could create the future the way you want it to be? What if it could be different this time?"

"I don't get it," she said. "How do I make others do what I want them to do?"

"That's the best part. You don't have to. All you have to do is focus on how you want things to go and, most importantly, feel how that would feel. And then, just believe that it can happen. You've already told me what you don't like about the hospital, which means now you know more clearly what you do want. So, tell me, how would you like it to go this time?"

"Well, first, I hate how long it takes to do all the paperwork before they even check you in," she said.

"You just did what most people do, Mom. You focused on what you don't want. How does it feel when you think about how long it takes?"

"It gives me a headache. It feels lousy," Mom replied.

"So, what's the opposite experience you'd like to have?"

"Okay, I want someone who enjoys their job and is really good at it. I want someone who can take a joke. I want to get the paperwork done in record time."

"And how does that feel," I asked.

"That feels great. It's actually exciting."

"Now, tell me about the perfect nurse. Go all out, because you can have anything you want. You create with your focused thoughts, and you want to really get the excitement going."

"I want to tell you about my room first. I want a room at the end of the hall that's quiet with a nice view. I want a good television that has controls that are easy to work and volume loud enough for me to hear easily. I want a comfortable bed with lots of warm blankets. I want nurses who are quick and know how to get the needles in the first time. Let's see, what else?"

"How about the personalities of the nurses?" I asked.

"Yeah. I want nurses who are efficient, and I want them to be quiet when I'm sleeping. I want nurses who get my humor and can joke with me. I want this hospital stay to feel easy. Oh, and one more thing. I want food with flavor."

"How do you feel now?" I asked.

"It feels like it's already happened. It feels good."

"Great. Now your job is to trust that it will happen. Let's go eat."

We ate a big meal at my brother's restaurant, and Mom took the full hour and a half to enjoy herself. Then we headed over to the hospital. As we walked to the reception area, I set my intention for this to be an easy and quick experience, that the person completing the paperwork was efficient, friendly, and fun.

"Hi, my name's Adrianna. I'll be completing your paperwork. Your room is ready, but we were expecting you about an hour ago."

"We stopped off for my last supper," Mom said.

Adrianna looked at me, not sure how to reply.

"Mom's been through this before and knows she won't be eating anything for a while," I said.

Adrianna visibly relaxed and said, "Oh, okay, good. Then you're familiar with these papers, so I'll skip all the explanation. While you fill these out, I'll order a wheelchair for you."

Mom and I split the paperwork and quickly completed the forms.

Adrianna returned and said, "There are two forms here that I'm required to go over with you. One is the DNR, and the other has to do with your living will."

"What's a DNR?" Mom asked.

"It means, do not resuscitate," Adrianna replied.

Still confused, Mom looked at me. "It basically means, if you croak, they won't resuscitate you," I said.

Adrianna's mouth fell open. She was speechless.

Then Mom and I started laughing and she relaxed. "Sorry, Adrianna, I should have warned you that Mom and I don't have the typical response to all of this that you're probably used to."

"So, what's this form about my will?" Mom asked.

"Do you have a living will that states how you want your affairs handled in case you aren't able to anymore?" Adrianna asked.

"No," Mom answered.

"This form just says that we offered you information on a living will. I have a standard form that you can take and fill out. You can either give it to me to put with your DNR, or you can keep it with your will."

"I don't have a will. No one's going to fight over my crap when I'm dead," Mom said.

"Right," I replied. "If there's any fighting, it'll go like this: 'You take it.' 'No, you take it.'"

This time Adrianna burst out laughing. "You guys are a breath of fresh air. I always have to be so careful about what I say. This was a relief. Thanks."

So, Mom received her first wish. We were done with the paperwork in record time. Then the wheelchair arrived, and as the staff member was wheeling Mom toward the elevators Mom yelled, "Out of my way, old woman coming through."

She was maintaining her focus on making this a better experience, and the momentum was building. As we exited the elevators and headed toward her room, Mom got her second wish. The staff member said, "We're way at the end of the hall."

Mom replied, "*We're* at the end of the hall? Are you staying in the room with me?"

He looked at me.

I shrugged and said, "Better you than me."

He said, "You better be nice to me, woman, or I'll put you in a room with no windows."

Mom laughed and was really happy to discover that her room was at the end of the hall with a view of the park across the street.

She stayed in the hospital three days longer than the doctor had told her, but she never complained about getting out. She lost sixty pounds of water while they had her on the intravenous diuretics. The doctor told me he had no idea it was so severe. It was twice what he expected. He was amazed at her recovery.

On the day she was to check out, I asked her to call me when she was ready. She told me the doctor would be by at ten o'clock to sign her out, but when I arrived to pick her up, she was still sitting on her bed in her hospital gown.

"What's going on?" I asked.

"The doctor just left. He was late, and now I'm waiting on the nurse to unhook me from all these machines."

Just then, an attractive male nurse in his thirties came into the room. "Well, I'm finally getting rid of you today," he said to Mom. He looked at me and asked her, "Is this the one you warned me about?"

"Yeah, she's no good."

We all laughed, and as he started unhooking the wires, I went into the restroom. Through the door I could hear him say, "Now, woman, I'm going to reach down the front of your gown. Do not grab my hand and hold it there like you did last time!"

I cracked up, not sure whether that was a joke or a prank she had actually pulled, and I didn't want to know. When I came back into the room they were both laughing at some private joke.

"While you get dressed, Mom, I'm going to go get something to drink. Do you want anything?"

"Do they have vodka? I'd like a screwdriver," she joked.

"She'll take water," the nurse said. "She's ornery enough sober!"

When I returned to the room, he had her in a wheelchair and was piling all her belongings on her lap. She had so much stuff, she couldn't see over the top of it.

"I'll carry something," I said.

"No, you won't," the nurse replied. "She gave me hell, and this is her punishment."

Before I could take anything from her, he started wheeling her down the hall. He got some speed going and jumped on the back of the wheelchair like it was a shopping cart. The nurses he passed in the hall just shook their heads and looked at me as if to say sorry.

When I caught up with them at the elevators, Mom was laughing like a kid and said, "Just wait until I get a chance to evaluate you. You'll be sorry."

"You don't scare me, woman," he replied.

He pushed her wheelchair into the elevator and placed her so that she was facing the corner. She kept trying to push away from the wall with her foot and he said, "You're in time out; just behave."

The other people in the elevator were completely confused about what was happening as he and I cracked up laughing.

When we finally made it out to the parking lot, Mom held him in a long hug and kissed him on the cheek.

His eyes watered as he said goodbye, then he smiled at me and said, "Good luck with that one!"

As I helped Mom into my Jeep for the ride home I asked her, "What was that all about?"

"I got all my wishes. I had a room at the end of the hall with a view of the park; I made friends with the lady who runs the lunchroom, and she snuck me some good food. I had a great television, and the nurses were wonderful."

"That male nurse is hilarious," I said.

"You know why? He used to be a scriptwriter for the show *Will and Grace*. When his mom died, he decided to change careers. Am I lucky or what?"

"It's not luck, Mom. You wrote the script, remember?"

Make your future dream a present fact by assuming the feeling of the wish fulfilled.

~ Neville

ඟඟඟ

Something More

It's through the contrast of the unwanted that you gain clarity for what you do want. You ask and it is given, unless you stop the momentum of the manifestation with contrary thoughts.

If you ask to have fun nurses but you keep thinking of all the times you had grumpy nurses and you don't believe there really are any fun nurses, the Law of Attraction can't buck the current of your vibration. You have free will, and the Law of Attraction responds to your vibration, not your words.

However, your words do have power, because the words you choose affect how you feel. And how you feel affects the vibrational signal you are sending out into the Universe. Words are a powerful indicator of what you are thinking and believing. And what you think and believe creates the life you are living.

That's why I had my mother speak to me about what she wanted and why I stopped her from telling me what she didn't want. If she had continued talking about all the times she had bad nurses and all the things she didn't like, how would she be feeling? Angry, frustrated, and fearful or happy, excited, and loved? Your emotions are always telling you where you're vibrating.

Remember, where your focus goes, energy flows. If you continue to focus on things you do not want, energy flows out into the Universe to magnetize things that match that vibration. So, you'll continue to attract things you do not want.

The good news is by being observant and intentional about what you speak and which thoughts you focus on, you can shift your life in dramatic ways. Look how quickly my mother manifested exactly what she wanted simply by speaking into her desire and feeling the excitement of it. Your words do matter, even the ones in your head that you don't speak, because they affect your vibrational signal.

ɞ ɞ ɞ

Something for You

We all want to be happy, and we believe the things we want in our life will bring us the happiness we seek. Yet, we have it backwards. We must feel happy first before we can receive our desires.

Yes, I know that seems crazy. Believe me, when I first heard this truth, I was confused and a little annoyed. How can I be happy when I don't have what I want?

The answer is simple but not always easy. Pay attention to the way you feel and deliberately choose thoughts that make you feel better. This shift in mindset from focusing on the positive rather than the negative takes consistent practice and present moment awareness.

Have you ever wondered why the news media and most consumer advertising focus mainly on what's wrong with the world and with us? Because they understand human nature. As humans, we give more importance and attention to negative experiences than to positive ones.

Right now, think of everything that went wrong yesterday. How many things did you come up with? Do you remember the details?

Now, think of everything good that happened yesterday. How many things did you remember? How about the details, were they easier or harder to recall?

If you're like most people, you probably remembered a lot more of the things that went wrong than right. And, most likely, you remember the details of the negative experiences more vividly than those of the positive experiences.

You can see this in action when you ask someone, "How was your day?" Rarely does anyone ramble on about all the wonderful things they experienced. Usually, it's a long list of all the negative things that happened along with all the details.

This tendency towards negativity is called negativity bias and is a built-in survival mechanism we inherited from our ancestors who had to gather food while avoiding deadly obstacles, like lions and tigers and bears. Those who were more aware of the dangers were most likely to survive.

Our ego is the subconscious repository for negativity bias and ensures our safety by vigilantly surveying the world for anything that may be dangerous or deadly. Since negative experiences are encoded much more strongly in the brain than positive experiences, we must consciously and consistently choose to focus on the positive aspects of our lives if we are to create the life of our dreams.

This doesn't mean we deny we have challenges or that we avoid our negative feelings. We simply acknowledge that these moments are temporary and do our best to think better feeling thoughts.

Your choices of action may be limited—but your choices of thought are not.

~ Abraham-Hicks

My mom was not happy when she realized she had to go back into the hospital. She was fearful and worried and was focused on the unpleasant things that happened in her past experiences. My goal was to have her use her imagination and think of positive outcomes to shift her vibration so she could create a better feeling experience. And it worked!

Even though we all face challenges in our lives, we can move through them with ease and grace if we learn how to use our imagination to raise our vibration so we are open to receive our desires.

Do you have a challenge in your life you would like to move through more gracefully? For this activity, you'll need your journal and a timer. I call this process Flip It +5.

Flip It +5

- Think of your challenge. What would you like to manifest regarding your challenge? At the top of your journal page, use this as your title, and be sure to make it a positive statement. For example, my mom's challenge was her hospital stay. What she wanted was a pleasant experience, so her title might be: Pleasant Stay at the Hospital.
- Next, draw a vertical line down the center of the page.
- On the left side of the line, list all the things you DON'T want regarding your challenge. (e.g. grumpy nurses, terrible food, isolation.) Because of negativity bias, it's usually easier to know what we don't want than what we do want.
- Looking at your list of unwanted, on the right side of the line FLIP IT and write the opposite. For example, if you wrote "grumpy nurses" on the left side, FLIP IT and write "happy nurses who have a good sense of humor" on the right side.
- Many people tend to write, "I want happy nurses," but wanting reflects an unmet need. It's important to claim it as if it's already done. Spend more time and be more descriptive writing what you desire, and imagine what it would feel like to have it.
- When you finish the right side, cross out the left side. This contrast served its purpose by giving you clarity of your desire. You might even write across the contrast list: "Thank you contrast for the clarity."

- On the bottom of the right side, write: "This or something better." The Universe always has your back. My mom imagined a nurse with a good sense of humor and got *something better*, something she would not have thought of or even believed possible, a writer from the comedy show *Will and Grace*.

- Set your timer for five minutes and read your list out loud several times until you can really feel your energy shift. Remember, it takes our minds much longer to encode the positive than the negative. When you read your list, be present and imagine it has already happened. After five minutes, if you feel a sense of relief, you have moved up the vibrational scale.

- The longer you stay in a positive vibe, the faster your desire will manifest. To maintain your positive shift in vibration, you can listen to uplifting music, walk in nature, or meditate on something happy from your past experiences.

You can use this FLIP IT +5 activity for anything you want to manifest. I also use it throughout the day whenever I notice my negative thoughts. I simply notice my negative thought and flip my thoughts to the positive by thinking of at least five positive things in my life.

Flip it. Flip it good!

CHAPTER 17

Butterflies Are Free to Fly

Happiness is a butterfly, which when pursued,
Is always just beyond your grasp, but which,
if you will sit down quietly,
May alight upon you.

~ Nathaniel Hawthorne

As I stood in my garden watering flowers, enjoying the warmth of the sunshine, hundreds of butterflies suddenly appeared and swirled around me, brushing against my skin like the breath of a whisper. I had never seen or felt anything like it. I stood there for several minutes, just enjoying their dance.

My thoughts wandered to the lyrics of a song from my teenage years, "Butterflies Are Free," and then to memories of my mother pleading, begging, and finally threatening me with the wrath of my father to coerce me out of the car and into the administration office to register for school.

Even though we moved almost every year, and I had always thought it would be nice to live in one place and experience having a friendship that lasted more than a few months, I wasn't ready for this. I had been a military brat all my life, and now that my father had retired, everything was changing. We were now civilians. I left a small school in Germany with a total of thirty eighth-grade students and was now registering in a public high school of over 3,000, and I knew *no one!*

It was my eighth school, my first month back in the United States, my first month being a civilian, and my first year of high school.

I have to admit, I expected high school to be awful, and it was. I was the tallest girl in the entire school, and I spoke with a funny accent since I'd been in Germany for almost two years. My two front teeth were broken from an early childhood accident, so I rarely smiled. I wasn't allowed to wear makeup, my mother cut my hair, and I wasn't allowed to dress like the other kids. It was the era of the seventies mini-skirt, and my skirts were below the knee.

So, no dances, no dates, no prom. The only reason I made it through high school was because of writing, art class, and two unconventional teachers.

My English teacher, Miss Marthes, showed me the power of words. Our class spent a whole semester analyzing the lyrics to popular songs such as "Nowhere Man" by the Beatles, "Bye, Bye Miss American Pie" by Don McLean, and "A Horse with No Name" by America. These songs all told a story and inspired me to start writing my own poetry.

My art teacher, Mrs. Frey, was unconventional as well. One day, she loaded our class on a school bus and took us to her ranch. We were scattered around her property sitting in the grass, sketching the nature around us: trees, horses, flowers. A butterfly landed on a flower I was drawing, and it was in that brief moment of escape and peaceful bliss that butterflies became my symbol of transformation, of hope for a happier life.

Like a butterfly stuck in a chrysalis, waiting for the perfect moment, I was waiting for the day I could burst forth and fly away and find my home.
~ Emme Rollins, *Dear Rockstar*

Today, whenever I want to raise my vibration and get to a better feeling place, all I do is focus on butterflies, and I'm there. And, when I'm there, butterflies show up.

Recently, I was reading a book titled *E-Squared* by Pam Grout, which offers do-it-yourself energy experiments to prove your thoughts create your own reality. So, I thought I'd play along and try one of her experiments.

Her challenge was to choose two things we intended to see in the next forty-eight hours. I chose white cars and, of course, butterflies.

The Theory: You impact the field and draw from it according to your beliefs and expectations.

The Question: Do I really see only what I expect to see?

The Hypothesis: If I decide to look for white cars and butterflies, I will find them.

By the following day, I had already forgotten about the experiment. I work from my home office and was so busy that I didn't even leave the house. So, the Universe had no way to deliver my desires to me.

The second day, I was on my way to my yoga class. As I was driving down the narrow, two-lane country road from our house in the Texas Hill Country, I saw a line of cars coming toward me. In the distance, they looked like a white snake slithering down the hill. It was unusual to see so many cars at once because few people traveled this road. But since no one could pass on the narrow road, and the first driver was driving so slowly, the eight white vehicles were almost bumper to bumper.

I was enjoying noticing that all the cars were white. But, since I had been preoccupied with the details of an upcoming trip, I'd forgotten about my experiment and didn't even make the connection that my choice was manifesting.

After my yoga class, I returned home, and as I pulled into the driveway, I noticed a swarm of butterflies at my garage door. I decided not to open the door for fear they would fly into the garage and get trapped, so I parked in the driveway and stepped out of my Jeep. And as the butterflies swarmed around me, I suddenly realized, "Oh my gosh, my white cars and butterflies!" They both showed up before the forty-eight-hour deadline!

Sometimes we get so caught up in the details of our everyday lives that we don't even notice when our dreams are being realized, even when the evidence is right under our noses.

We live on autopilot, focused on somewhere other than the present moment.

This experiment also reminded me that we can intend and believe, but we must also be out in the world to receive.

And, just when you think this is the end of this story, it isn't.

I had just finished writing the first draft of this chapter and was sitting at my desk with the curtains drawn to reduce the glare of the sun on my computer screen. I was in the process of printing my airline tickets for a trip the following day. For some unknown reason, my computer and printer were not communicating. I tried for several minutes to print, and nothing worked.

My first thought was *What the heck?* But knowing that everything is always working out for me, and knowing that there are no coincidences, my second thought was *That's interesting. There's something fabulous about to happen.*

A few minutes later, after sitting quietly in meditation and breathing deeply, I was able to shift my energy to a place of peace and trust. I returned to my computer, randomly tapped various combinations of keys, and the printer started working again. So, with tickets in hand, I walked outside into our breezeway that connects our main house to my office.

Butterflies, hundreds of butterflies, were flying up from the valley below our house. They danced around me, hovered for a moment, then drifted over the roof of our breezeway. For ten minutes, they continued floating up from the valley as I stood with tears streaming down my face in appreciation for the reminder of how much I am loved.

I like knowing that as I look for the best things around me where I am, those things become more prevalent in my experience. It is fun to know that things are always working out for me, and as I watch for the evidence of that… I see more evidence of that every day.
~ Abraham-Hicks, *Money and the Law of Attraction*

ᘓᘓᘓ

Something More

Little miracles are happening all around us. My butterfly miracle was an example of how the Universe conspires to surprise and delight us. If I had printed out my ticket on the first try, I would have missed the thousands of butterflies that flew over my house.

And, If I had allowed the malfunction of my printer to frustrate and irritate me, I would not have been in vibrational alignment with my miracle of butterflies. Most likely, I would have stayed in my office grumbling, griping, and fidgeting with my computer and never stepped out into the courtyard in time to see them. A simple pause and shift in focus made all the difference.

Which thought feels better: "What the heck?" Or "That's interesting. There's something fabulous about to happen."

Can you FEEL the difference in your body? One feels constricted, and one feels open. One feels like a closed door, the other like an open door inviting in all that is good. Your emotional guidance system gives immediate feedback letting you know how near or far you are from realizing your desire.

Whenever you feel frustration, anger, fear, or resentment around anything in your life, you block your creations from manifesting. For example, if you continuously focus on the lack of money and feel frustrated and angry, not only will your abundance be blocked but also any desires around relationships, health, or any other desire you hold. Why? Because you're tuned into the frequency of lack.

Don't worry. This doesn't mean you must be perfectly happy all the time to manifest your miracles. In fact, it's impossible as a human being to always be happy. We're wired to always want *something more*. Desire is what gets us up in the morning. Besides, without experiencing fear, anger, and resentment, how would we know love, joy, and appreciation?

Your work is simply to increase your happiness set point, little by little, day by day, until you return to your natural state of joy and well-being. Mastery takes practice until the new neural pathways are firmly established.

Did you know that your brain has over 100 trillion neural connections? The thoughts you think and the feelings you feel strengthen this circuitry in your brain. There is a lot of neural power right at your fingertips once you shift out of autopilot and become a deliberate creator.

For example, when I was trying to print my airline tickets, my first reaction was frustration. Yet, because I have practiced shifting my mindset for so long, the neural pathways of looking for the positive in every situation were dominant, and I was able to shift my perspective in seconds. It has become almost automatic. That's why, often, as soon as I have a thought about a desire, it manifests like a miracle, whether it's white cars and butterflies, a leopard-print top, or a private jet ride from a stranger.

Don't get me wrong, I still have my moments of frustration and sadness, anger, and regret like everyone. The difference is those moments are the exception not the rule. My daily focus on gratitude, my trust that things are always working out for me, my consistent practice of flipping my focus from negative thoughts to positive allows me to create miracles for myself with ease. And you can too.

Diffusing stress is vital to creating and rewiring neural pathways because when you are stressed, your brain will defer to the strongest neural pathways out of survival and path of least resistance. That's why during stress you don't have access to newly formed neural networks. They haven't been practiced enough, so the emotional intensity of the stress response easily overrides our new attempt to focus on the positive or to create new habits.

If you notice your thoughts are primarily geared to look for the negative (negativity bias strikes again), you have well-established neural pathways that feel comfortable and familiar. And since the ego loves the comfortable and familiar, it will require awareness, intention, and a dedicated practice to live a life of joy.

Neural pathways are like a well-worn bike path through a field. To increase your happiness set point, you must take the road less traveled and create new pathways. And like a new bike path, it will feel bumpy at times and will require repeatedly traveling the new pathway to make it a smoother ride. Eventually, you will more easily default to your new positive perspective, and the old pattern of negativity will fade into the background like an old bike path overgrown from lack of use.

So, how do you diffuse stress, change your neural pathways, and increase your happiness level? One of the most powerful tools for manifesting change is meditation because rewiring your brain happens within the relationship of mind, body, and soul (breath).

෬෬෬

Something for You

Miracle: an extraordinary event manifesting Divine intervention in human affairs

How do you create miracles in your life? First, by believing that miracles happen every day, and second, by understanding you are the miracle maker. You are of the Divine living a human experience. Everything you need to create a miraculous life is not outside of you, it's already within you.

However, most people are not aware they are recycling yesterday's old thoughts ninety-five percent of the time. And, because they are living on autopilot, their life never changes, no matter how hard they try.

When we live on autopilot reacting to the world around us, we live in stress mode. When we are under stress, our body becomes tense and our breath becomes quick and shallow. We cannot be in stress mode and creative mode at the same time.

Meditation is a tool to interrupt the mind of its obsessive thinking and calm the nervous system. In meditation, we retract from the outside world to connect to the Soulful Self through our breath. When you breathe deeply into the core of your body, you energize and enliven your Soulful Self, the real you, because you are the breath itself.

On a typical day, I usually meditate twenty to thirty minutes first thing in the morning before my feet hit the ground. And during the day for a short two to five minutes if I notice that I'm not feeling aligned or things aren't moving forward easily. In the evening, I meditate when I go to bed by listening to an app on my cell phone. I'm usually asleep within three minutes.

When I first started meditating, belly breathing felt unnatural, and I could only inhale to the count of three. Five minutes felt like forever. Today, I inhale and exhale to the count of ten, belly breathing feels natural, and thirty minutes in meditation feels like five minutes.

It's important to start small; otherwise, you'll get frustrated and discouraged. Start with five minutes of meditation and increase the time slowly, but only when you're comfortable. Try to meditate a few minutes every day if possible. Meditation is simple once you get into the habit of doing it. You can't get this wrong.

Yes, thoughts will pop in. That is normal, and it's the reason you want to meditate. Embrace the experience without judgment and love into it. Remember, you have over 60,000 thoughts a day. The purpose of meditation isn't to stop the thoughts, it's to shift the focus of your mind to your body and your breath to build a better relationship, a bridge, between your Soulful Self and your thinking mind.

A consistent meditation practice, ideally, twenty minutes a day, will help you relax the body and quiet the mind so you can shift out of autopilot, hear the wisdom of your soul, release resistance, raise your vibration, and open to a life of miracles.

The past is just a story that cannot be changed. The future is simply a projection of your thoughts and is not yet reality. The present moment, where all your power to create resides, requires the integration of mind, body, and breath. So, let's switch off your autopilot for a moment and shift into miracle-making mode.

Mindful Meditation
- Sit comfortably where you won't be disturbed.
- Set a timer for five minutes.
- Close your eyes.
- Relax your tongue on the floor of your mouth. This sends a signal to your nervous system to relax.
- Purposefully relax all muscle tension in your body. Relax your face, your neck, your shoulders. Relax your back, your arms, wrists, and hands. Relax your hips, legs, and feet.
- Take a few breaths and gently follow the breath. Notice if your shoulders rise as you inhale. If they do, relax the

shoulders and focus on taking belly breaths. Expand the belly on the inhale and contract the belly on the exhale. The shoulders should stay relaxed and only rise after the belly is full.

- Now, begin to purposely extend the breath, taking a slow inhale to the count of four, six, or eight. Then exhale to the same number of counts. For example, if you inhale to the count of four, also exhale to the count of four. Take deep breaths, and let it be easy. As you continue to belly breathe, you may notice that you are able to extend the breath a little more.

- Over time, (days, weeks, months) you'll work your way to slowing the breath down to ten or more counts. Wherever you're starting is perfect. The main idea is to inhale and exhale for the same number of counts and to FEEL and follow the breath as it travels through the body.

- Inevitably, thoughts will enter your mind. Just notice them and say, "Later Gator! Right now, just breathe." Or, imagine the thoughts floating away inside a bubble. Then return to counting your breaths.

- Continue deep breathing and counting until the timer goes off.

- Gently open your eyes and notice how your body feels.

By practicing this simple meditation three or four times a week, you'll stop the constant flow of thoughts so you can experience that deep state of presence beyond the thinking mind. When you lovingly slow down your thoughts and breathe deeply, you connect to your inner wisdom.

Your authentic self, your Soulful Self, is pure love. To live a life of miracles requires you to switch off the autopilot of the protective personality (ego) and take back the controls. By training yourself to meditate daily, you will stay connected to your authentic self, reset your happiness set point, and create miracles in your life. It's as easy as breathe, one, two, three.

Transformation, like a butterfly emerging from its chrysalis, requires that we shed our old habits, patterns, and perspectives to emerge into this world as our authentic self.

~ Kat Wells

CHAPTER 18

Star-Bucks

*As you set a financial goal, it is not only about the expansion for
yourself; it's about the expansion of all of those who are involved in
that which you are about. In other words, it creates this nucleus,
this machine that allows so many to begin to thrive along with
you. It's much bigger than finances.*

~ Abraham-Hicks

"Are you sure?" she asked. "It's a large order: grande mocha, apple-bran muffin, chai tea, everything-with-cheese bagel, birthday-cake pop, and a chocolate smoothie."

As I looked in my rearview mirror, I could see a young man in a black pickup truck wearing a baseball cap and sunglasses. Behind him, I glimpsed a small child waving her hands in the air as if trying to get her point across.

"I'm sure," I replied. "And keep the change."

The barista smiled as she handed me my grande vanilla latte and a cup of water for my mom.

I quickly pulled out of the drive-through window lane and into traffic, wanting to disappear and let the gift be a mystery. It's always more fun that way. Being anonymous.

"Why did you do that?" Mom asked as she readjusted her seatbelt.

"Because it's fun. I love starting someone's day off on a positive note. When they pull up to the window and are told that a stranger just paid their bill, not only do they feel good, but their good feelings affect everyone around them."

"But aren't you literally throwing money out the window?" she asked.

"I like to look at it as throwing a pebble into a pond and creating a ripple effect." I replied. "The barista at Starbucks gets a triple dose of good feelings because she received a large tip from me, witnessed a random act of kindness, and gets to experience the surprise and delight of her next customer. And the barista's good feelings will flow over into her day, affecting her interactions with her customers and coworkers."

"I think I understand what you mean. So, the man and his little girl behind you will have a fun story to share, and since they are in a good mood, it will affect others whom they encounter today," Mom added.

"Yes, and who knows how far the ripples will reach. To me that's priceless."

I smiled to myself, realizing how far I had come from the little girl who used to watch her mother hide envelopes of money behind the paint-by-number pictures that hung on the walls in our living room. She didn't want Dad spending what little money we had on alcohol.

I remember once eating oatmeal-and-raisin cookies for every meal for a few days before payday because oatmeal was the only thing we had left in the house. Mom tried to make it seem like a treat. She always did the best she could.

"I think that's very sweet of you, honey, but what if you need that money later?" Mom asked.

"It always comes back to me multiplied," I said. "Last week, I was sitting in the drive-through line at Starbucks debating on whether to give the cashier a fifteen-dollar tip or pay for the person's order behind me. I decided to do both, pay for the person behind me and give the rest to the barista for a tip.

"As I pulled up to the payment window with a twenty-dollar bill in my hand, the cashier smiled at me and said, 'It's already paid for. The lady in front of you paid for your order.'"

Mom joked, "I guess the bucks were in the stars for you that day. Star. Bucks. Get it?"

"That's really bad, Mom."

"I know. So, what did you do when she told you it was already paid?" she asked.

"I told her that I had intended to do the same thing, pay for the customer behind me and give her a ten-dollar tip. And since I didn't have to pay for my coffee, she was getting a fifteen-dollar tip."

"What did she do?" Mom asked.

"Before she could say anything, another barista standing behind her leaned through the window and said, 'You don't have to do that.' And I said, 'You don't have to be cheerful and efficient and kind. But you are, and I appreciate you.'"

You cannot get through a single day without having an impact on the world around you. What you do makes a difference, and you have to decide what kind of difference you want to make.

~ Jane Goodall

ададад

Something More

My mom's life experiences made her fearful of not having enough money to take care of her young family. So, watching me buy food for strangers who weren't in need seemed careless to her. Unfortunately, I inherited my parents' lack mindset and struggled financially for many years until I discovered the truth.

What you believe, you receive. If you believe you must work hard to receive money, that will be your experience. If you believe this is an abundant, loving Universe and there is plenty for everyone, that will be your experience.

Be honest. When you think about money, how do you feel? Excitement and freedom, or worry and concern? One of the challenges in receiving more money into our lives is that society, in general, believes there's a limited amount and that we must work hard for it. Sound familiar?

Regardless of where you are in your relationship with money, whether you simply want enough to pay your bills or you are debt free, there's always *something more* available to you.

Yet, if you believe you must guard your money because you fear no more is coming, it's like holding your breath because you fear there's no more oxygen available. There's always more, but a fear in lack won't allow it in. Just like holding your breath doesn't allow you to breathe in the oxygen always available to you, holding onto your money out of fear doesn't allow room for more to flow to you.

I understand that may be hard to believe if you're struggling to pay your bills. Many years ago, when I was going through bankruptcy, my ego mind made up all kinds of horror stories that kept me up at night. And then I realized they were just stories. They were not real.

I also discovered that what happened wasn't personal. I wasn't being punished. I wasn't unworthy. Once I chose to look at my situation through the eyes of love, I realized my ex-husband and his business partner simply made mistakes. And bankruptcy wasn't a problem, it was the solution.

The truth is, we live in a loving, abundant Universe, and our greatest strength is the ability to love and be positive in the face of challenge. By shifting my perspective of reality from one of lack to one of gratitude and abundance, not only did I eventually create financial freedom for myself, but more importantly, I discovered how resilient, courageous, and loving I can be in the face of challenges.

The soul knows abundance is our birthright. The ego fears lack because it doesn't have the capacity to act outside of what has been programmed and experienced. That's why many would argue that paying five dollars for a cup of coffee is a waste of money. It's why my mom questioned what she perceived as irresponsibility.

Spending money at Starbucks doesn't take away from others, nor is it a waste of money. Money is simply one form of energy exchange that fuels our economy and supports the lives of people all around the world. Did you know that around 125 million people worldwide depend on coffee for their livelihoods?

Every dollar I spend at Starbucks allows so many others to thrive along with me. The owner and employees of Starbucks and their families. The farmers who cared for and grew the coffee plants and whose sweat harvested the crops. The crew who spent weeks on a ship that carried the coffee beans across the ocean. The long-haul truckers who drove hundreds and thousands of miles to deliver the beans to the packaging plant. The workers who risk their lives in the oilfield for the fuel. The insurance, packaging, and advertising companies.

The list could go on for pages. Every dollar you spend is about the expansion of all those involved. It's the ripple effect of prosperity and love. So, the more abundance you allow into your life, the more love you have to share with the world.

On a recent trip to Starbucks, I had the pleasure of experiencing the ripple effect of love and abundance created by my simple gesture of anonymously paying the tab for the car behind me. The owner of the coffee shop happened to be working at the drive-through window and shared with me that whenever I come by, they keep track of how many customers pay my gift forward to the next car. She said, "So far, the longest run we've had is twenty-three cars!"

Our true essence is love. When we open our heart and share with others, it not only expands our capacity to receive, it also allows others to connect to their heart, and together we bring more love into this world we call home.

ᘓᘓᘓ

Something for You

The truth is the only thing holding anyone back from their desires is a pattern of belief in lack and limitation. And beliefs are simply thoughts we keep thinking. Those thoughts keep attracting circumstances that are a vibrational match to lack and limitation. You can't be in a feeling of lack and allow abundance. Those two vibrations are different frequencies.

The good news is you have the ability to begin a new pattern of thought, to create new beliefs, and to achieve a new vibration, thereby changing your point of attraction to one of abundance. And it's easier than you think. Simply acting abundant allows you to feel abundant. And when you feel prosperous, you are in vibrational harmony with your desire.

Recently, I was in Indianapolis for a training seminar and stayed in a hotel near the event. The hotel happened to be next door to a Mayo Clinic treatment center. Many of the guests at the hotel were receiving treatments for health issues at the clinic.

One evening, as I sat by myself eating dinner in the hotel restaurant, I noticed an older couple in their late seventies sitting huddled together in conversation at a nearby table. They appeared worried and tired, so I decided to anonymously pay for their dinner to lift their spirits. I discretely asked my server to add their meal to my dinner bill and to keep it anonymous.

The following morning, I stopped for breakfast at the hotel restaurant. While I ate, the older couple from the previous night approached the counter to place their order. The woman caught my eye and walked over to my table. "Excuse me, I believe you're the person who paid for our dinner last night," she said.

"Well, yes. But, it was supposed to be anonymous," I replied.

"Oh, it was," she said. "I just somehow knew it was you. I'm so glad I saw you this morning so I could tell you how much it meant to us. My husband got some bad news about his health last night, and we were praying for a sign that everything would be okay. Your generosity was the answer to our prayer. We are so grateful. You gave us back our hope."

You never know how you might change someone's life with a simple smile or a kind gesture. And, you don't need to be a millionaire or a superstar to make a difference in this world.

After the couple left the restaurant, I motioned to the server to bring me my bill. Instead, she brought me a receipt. "Your breakfast is on the house," she said. "Your kindness lifted everyone's spirits. Thank you so much."

When we share our abundance with others we expand our capacity to receive. There is a caveat, however, a nuance that is extremely important to understand that most people don't realize affects their ability to manifest the abundance they desire. When you share your abundance with others, let it be from soul love, not from the ego's need for acknowledgement, praise, or reciprocation.

When we give with the expectation of getting something in return, even a compliment, we are often in the vibration of lack. When we give from the spirit of generosity and open heartedness, we are in the vibration of joy, freedom, and love, which is the vibration of abundance.

That's why I love Anonymous Acts of Prosperity and Love, or what I call AAPL (apple) for short. Random Acts of Kindness on steroids. When we share our abundance anonymously, we bypass the ego's need for acknowledgement or reciprocation. And giving anonymously feels less like charity to the receiver and more like a miracle. Plus, it's more fun! It's like playing Santa Claus, the Easter Bunny, and the Tooth Fairy all rolled into one.

When we give to others purely from the heart, the energy creates a ripple effect that can be felt by others even when you give anonymously. For example, can you think of someone who, without even speaking a word, makes you feel better just by being in their presence? That's because our nervous system acts as an antenna tuned to and responding to the magnetic fields produced by the hearts of others.

The heart's electromagnetic energy field is 5,000 times greater than the energy field of the brain. When you act from love and compassion, you literally touch the hearts of others. What makes Anonymous Acts of Prosperity and Love even more exciting is that not only does the direct recipient receive the benefit, but also those in their proximity and those in your proximity. It's energetic heart communication. It's the gift that keeps on giving.

If you'd like to expand your ability to receive abundance in your life, simply begin by acting abundant through Random Acts of Kindness and Anonymous Acts of Prosperity and Love. And remember, a life of abundance isn't just about money and wealth. Abundance comes in many forms: relationships, ideas, creativity, health, laughter, joy, love, gratitude. You don't have to give money to share your abundance; simply give what you can from where you are.

An AAPL a day sends abundance your way!

Whether you choose to do Random Acts of Kindness or Anonymous Acts of Prosperity and Love, remember to do it without the need for acknowledgement or recognition. Do it for love.

Making a quick list of five or more things that inspire you to share your abundance creates focused intention and will make this new habit of acting abundant even easier for you. Some of activities below cost a few dollars, some are free. Some are anonymous, some are not. Hopefully, as you read through the list, you'll find some ideas that inspire you and some that stimulate ideas of your own. Use your talents and be creative.

- If you're in a drive-through at a coffeeshop, restaurant, pharmacy, or dry cleaners, pay $10 toward the bill of the car behind you. (I had to put this one in.)
- If you have a garden, anonymously share your harvest by leaving a bag of goodies on the doorstep of a neighbor.
- If your neighbor's trash and recycling bins are still out after they've been emptied, anonymously move them closer to their house to make it easy for them to put them away.
- Smile at strangers. It may be the only smile they receive all day.

- Say please and thank you with sincerity while looking in the recipient's eyes and using their name (if you know it). Most people in the service industry feel invisible. For example, have you ever had the experience of ordering at a restaurant and later, when you need to find the waiter, can't remember what he looks like?
- Open doors for others and let them pass through first. And when they say, "Thank you," respond by saying, "You are very welcome," with sincerity.
- Send flowers anonymously with a simple card that says, "You matter" or "You are loved."
- If you see someone who is having a bad day, whether it's the guy on the side of the road changing a flat tire or a salesperson dealing with an angry customer, take a few deep breaths, connect with your heart, and send them a silent prayer for ease and peace. They will feel it even though they don't know why (the heart's electromagnetic energy field).
- Collect small, smooth rocks and, using paint pens, write inspirational words (Love, Joy, Peace, Calm) or phrases or draw pictures on one side. On the other side, paint 4U. Then leave them randomly on pathways when you're on a walk, in someone's garden, on a chair in a restaurant. You get the idea. Be creative.
- If you're artistic, create a small, uplifting illustration and add a few words of inspiration. Make copies and anonymously leave them wherever you go: in a basket at the supermarket, at the checkout counter when the

clerk isn't looking, on bulletin boards, inside a library book, etc.

- Volunteer in your community. There are hundreds of opportunities to share your love and give back.

Challenge yourself to give something every day for a week and notice what happens. It can be as simple as saying, "Thank you," or spending a couple minutes sending out a prayer of love and well-being to another.

As you give to others, you will notice more abundance flowing into your life. It's important to acknowledge these gifts and to be a gracious receiver.

Have you ever had the experience of giving a gift that wasn't acknowledged or received with appreciation? Did you feel inspired to give the person another gift? The Universe responds to your vibration, whether you are the giver or the receiver. When you give with love and receive with grace, you are telling the Universe, "More please!" And we all know, there's always *something more*!

CHAPTER 19

Faux Pas

What you believe to be true will be true for you,
and so your life will be.

~ Kat Wells

I couldn't stop her. I tried to interrupt a couple of times, but she was having none of it. It all started innocently enough. She had been referred to me by a neighbor. I wanted a bid to repaint a television armoire, and she stopped by to drop off a book of sample finishes.

"So, how long have you been painting faux finishes?" I asked.

"Several years," Susie replied, as she adjusted her chunky turquoise necklace and straightened her long, starched white shirt.

Her porcelain skin was a beautiful contrast to her dark hair pulled back into a tight bun. She wore black leggings and crystal-studded flats.

"I was expecting you to be in a paint-splattered work shirt and sneakers. Aren't you on your way to Jan's house to finish her bathroom walls?" I asked.

"My painting clothes are in the car," she said. "I just change shirts and shoes, and I'm ready to go."

"If you're like me, your work shirt is covered in layers of paint," I said.

"Oh, do you paint too?" she asked, looking surprised.

"Yes, I did faux finishing for a few years when I had an interior decorating business. Have you heard of the Vineyards Restaurant?"

"Yes!" she said. "I've got a story about that place. You'll never guess what happened to me."

I could tell by the tone of her voice and the tension in her body that this was not something she would share if she knew who I was.

Even though she was making eye contact with me and I was trying to stop her, she wasn't really seeing me. She was watching the movie of her story in her mind.

"I was working at this newly built, ten-thousand-square-foot home," Susie said as she laid her sample book on my breakfast bar. "The homeowners hadn't moved in yet, and the builder was letting people drop by to see his work. I was standing on a ladder, painting the living room walls when this woman walked in and started asking me questions," she added.

"She told me her husband owned Vineyards Restaurant, and they were building a new location. She thought the finish

I was applying on the walls would work with their restaurant design and asked me about my fees."

Again, I tried to interrupt Susie, but she was talking so fast that I couldn't get a word in.

"So, I gave her my business card," Susie said, "and told her what I charged per square foot. She told me she'd get back to me, but months went by, and I never heard from her."

"Then," she continued, "my friend, Debbie and I were going out to dinner one night, and she suggested that we try a new restaurant near her home called Vineyards. When we walked in, I was shocked to see my faux finish on their walls! Can you believe it!" she exclaimed.

"They copied my finish and hired someone else to do it. There had to be over seven thousand square feet of walls in that restaurant. People are always taking from me. Even that rich guy who built that huge house I was working in never paid me. That's why rich people have money. They're always taking from others. I don't know how much longer I can do this work. I'm getting older, and it's hard on me. See this scar? I had to have surgery on my neck because of all the stress from painting ceilings. It's just not fair!"

I reached over, touched her arm, looked into her eyes, and asked, "May I share something with you that may make you feel better about all that?"

With hesitation in her voice, she said, "Okay."

"Vineyards is my brother's restaurant, and I am the one who faux finished those walls along with my friend Sandy. I help my brother decorate all his restaurants. Sandy created several sample boards for my brother to choose from."

Before I could finish, she interrupted and said, "Yes, but his wife copied my finish, and I lost a big paying job. I looked closely at the finish in the restaurant, and she had to have copied the three-step process I developed. It's the only way to get that look."

"I never knew my sister-in-law talked with you," I said. "And she'll be the first to admit she knows nothing about painting or decorating. She just tries to help my brother by locating quality people to do finish work for him. Besides, Sandy and I didn't even live here at the time the restaurant was built. I brought the samples with me on one of my consultation trips to town, and he chose one. I never saw your work. And you might be surprised to know that the faux finish we used was a one-step process."

"What? There's no way that's possible," she replied.

"Not too long ago, I thought the same thing. But Sandy owns a nontoxic paint manufacturing company. She's created stains and gels that blend so nicely with paint, that we simply used rough brushes and a mixture of paint, stain, and glaze medium to apply one layer.

"Thank goodness, because it still took us over a week on scaffolds and scissor lifts to paint that huge place. Using a three-step process would have been cost prohibitive for my brother, not to mention time consuming and exhausting.

"I have the formula on my bulletin board in my office. If you'd like, I can share it with you and introduce you to Sandy.

She loves sharing her techniques, and it might make your work easier on your body."

Susie just stood with her arms crossed, looking at me.

"I just didn't want you to feel bad because you believed someone had taken something from you," I added.

"Well, I still can't believe that a one-step process looks exactly like my three-step process. And that homeowner not paying me wasn't the first time someone did that to me," she said.

All I could say was, "Let's look at your sample book and see what might work for my television armoire."

We had a long conversation about various options, yet with everything I selected, she complained about how hard it would be or said it wouldn't look good with my decor.

What could have been a simple job was now becoming complicated and expensive. I thanked her for her ideas, and Susie agreed to return at the end of the week with a couple of sample boards.

After she cancelled two follow-up consultations with me, I knew she wasn't interested in doing the job. When she called to reschedule for the third time, I said, "Thank you, Susie, for all your input and suggestions. My husband and I took a closer look at the quality of the cabinet and agreed that it wasn't worth the investment of your time and energy. Can I pay you a consultation fee?"

"No, that's not necessary. It's probably a good thing you changed your mind because I'm so busy now that it would be a couple months before I could get started on it," Susie replied.

A few days later, my friend, Linda, called and asked me to go shopping to help her pick out some new furniture for her living room.

"Yes, I'd love to go," I said. "I need to look for a new television armoire."

We went to several stores and took measurements of furniture pieces Linda thought would work for her living room. But I didn't see any television armoires that even came close to what I had pictured in my mind. And I knew the perfect piece was waiting for me. Somewhere.

When we returned to her house to look at her space and measure for her new pieces, Linda asked, "Do you know anyone who might want to buy my old living room furniture?"

"Are you selling your television armoire too?" I asked.

"Yes, I've had it for years. Are you interested in buying it? I thought you'd want something new."

"Linda, it's new to me, and it's exactly what I've been looking for!"

You are the vibrational writers of the script of your life, and everyone else in the Universe is playing the part that you have assigned to them.
~ Esther and Jerry Hicks-Abraham

ᘰᘰᘰ

Something More

Our stories are a construct of our perceptions, which shift and change over time. Susie had an opportunity to ease her physical stress by learning a new painting technique and to receive more abundance into her life by acknowledging that people want to pay her for her time and talent. All she had to do was be willing to let go of her old story.

Truth: the property of being in accord with fact or reality

We think and we believe our thoughts to be true. And from our current perspective, they are. But what if we change our story? When we change our story, we change our reality. When we change our reality, our truth also changes. So, truth is subjective.

I didn't argue with Susie because she wasn't wrong. From her perspective, she was right. I simply offered her new information so she could choose to shift her beliefs and feel better about the situation.

Whenever we try to push our "rightness" towards another, no matter how right we believe we are, we create resistance and hold the door closed to receiving what we desire. We must allow others their perspectives if we want to live a joyful life. That doesn't mean we have to agree with them, we just have to "Let It Be," as the Beatles' song reminds us.

We humans have powerful imaginations. We dream things up, and we project stories onto people and situations to make sense of our world. We imagine what other people think of us, what they say about us, what they may do to us. We create a whole story, like Susie did about the faux finish at the restaurant, and we believe our stories and suffer for them.

Rather than address the cause of her suffering, which was simply a misperception, Susie tried to make life fit her misperception. Why? Somewhere in her subconscious, she holds a belief that life is a struggle, work is hard, and people always want to take from her. So, her ego is constantly scanning her environment looking for information to support her beliefs. We only see what we expect to see. She didn't know she created the life she is living by clinging to her stories and continuing to focus on them as if they are truth.

When our story continues to cause us pain or suffering, it's a signal from the soul to look at our story from a fresh perspective, otherwise we remain a victim and a more joyful life is not accessible. We are the storytellers of our lives, and we have free will to tell a hero's story or a victim's story.

So, why are we so attached to our stories? The mind writes stories to make sense of our world. Our stories allow us to see the patterns in life, which helps us to feel safe. We share our stories to belong and to be part of a shared history. And sometimes we share stories to justify our situation and gain sympathy.

Our beliefs are based on past experiences and are simply perspectives that our ego found useful at the time. They are not absolute truth. These partial, incomplete, and partly false beliefs become deeply entrenched in our long-term memory and run on autopilot in our subconscious.

The subconscious mind contains the library of our stories catalogued according to our personal perspective. Our ego is the keeper of the library, the librarian, and likes everything organized and categorized. The problem is the librarian wants only the stories it agrees with in the library. And when we try to bring in new stories that are contrary to what is already organized and catalogued, the librarian shushes us and tell us to be quiet.

The librarian fears change and the unknown. What if the new story doesn't end well? What if there's something scary in the new story that might cause pain? Even worse, what if the new story contradicts what we thought was truth? Even if the old stories are painful, at least they are predictable. We know how they end.

What the librarian has forgotten is the stories aren't real. In the story, we don't see things as they are, only how we perceive them to be. But if we remember to come back to the present moment, we see that we were safe all along. It was just a story. And we have free will to reach for a new, better feeling story. We own the library!

ᘓᘓᘓ

Something for You

Can I share a secret with you? No two realities are the same, nor will they ever be. We are each unique and important to making this a diverse and interesting world in which to live. Yet, we spend so much of our precious time arguing over whose reality is the truth. Have you noticed that getting complete consensus on anything is an impossible endeavor?

Remember when our ancestors thought the world was flat? In their perspective, this was truth, and they lived their lives afraid to go too far from shore in fear they would fall off the planet. That was until someone challenged the belief by sailing beyond what others feared, and a whole new world opened to be explored. Simply by challenging one belief. By asking one question: What if?

Being "right" means we can venture no further than our limited view. Our ancestors didn't know what they didn't know. The unknown wasn't safe, so they lived limited lives because fear didn't allow space for curiosity. When we are curious, we open to new possibilities.

Our truth is always changing. Once we recognize it's not an absolute, then we don't have to spend our lives defending our perspective. Have you ever noticed that when you tell a story it changes depending on who you're sharing it with? If we don't like the story of our life, we have the power to change it.

It's okay to be skeptical, but learning to listen without judging the story or the storyteller gives us freedom to question our current beliefs and create new ones that support a life of joy, happiness, and adventure.

What if Susie had allowed herself to be open to a new version of her story? If she had been curious and asked me for more information, she would have received a new faux-paint formula for free. The one-step finish would have saved her time, money, and the wear and tear on her body.

It would have allowed her to grow her business and make more money by working less. She had the answer to her desires right in front of her, but her librarian shushed her and she complied.

It takes courage to be honest with yourself, to see the truth about how you write your story, and to be open to a new perspective Yet, if you can shift your perspective for just a moment and ask, "What if...?" you open to a new version of your story that changes your beliefs. And *presto-change-o*, just like magic, your suffering disappears.

What If ...

Try this experiment with a current situation in your life that you struggle with.

- In your journal, write the story of this situation as if you're talking to your best friend or writing them a letter. Don't edit yourself or try to sound diplomatic. Tell it like it is! Allow your feelings to be expressed.
- Next, set your timer for three minutes, close your eyes, and take long, deep belly breaths. Imagine this story as a symbol. Now put this symbol inside a snow globe filled with snowflakes shaped like hearts. This snow globe is filled with your loving energy, and as you shake your snow globe, your story is transformed. You won't know what your new story will look like until the snow has settled.
- Now, open your eyes and consider the following questions about your story through the eyes of love:

- ◦ What if this situation is in my favor?
- ◦ What if the opposite of what I believed is true?
- ◦ What if I looked at this from a different perspective?
- ◦ What if I looked at this from the other person's perspective?
- ◦ What if I could have this any way I like?
- ◦ Next, rewrite your story from this new perspective of soul love, knowing that you are a radiant being of light and love, graced with an innate power to create the life of your dreams.

Be curious, be courageous, be a conscious creator. And give your librarian (ego) a new job description!

CHAPTER 20

Siri-ously

It is not your job to make something happen—your work is to
simply determine what you want.

~ Esther and Jerry Hicks-Abraham

I'm executor of Mom's estate, and I'm so angry at my siblings, I don't want to give them anything!" my client, Margie, shouted into the phone.

"Is that an option?" I asked.

"Actually, it is. Mom gave me full power of attorney to distribute what she had," she replied.

"And would that make you feel better?"

She sighed and said, "No, that's not who I really am. But it did feel good for just a moment to realize I could if I wanted to."

"And," I added, "We always have the power of choice. So, what is it that you do want?"

"I want clarity. I want a higher-level perspective on what action to take. But I can't get over my anger at them," Margie said.

"What if anger is just resistance to the truth you already know? What could you do to access that higher perspective, that clarity?" I asked.

"I guess I could meditate, but it's so hard to have no thoughts when so much is going on. There's so much to do."

"Quieting your mind is a powerful form of meditation, but it's not the only way. The whole purpose of meditation is to release resistance so that you feel better. And sometimes trying to quiet your mind isn't the path of least resistance."

"What do you mean?" Margie asked.

"I've discovered that guided meditation works better for me when I have trouble quieting my mind. Would you like me to share with you one that I use to see if it helps?" I asked.

"Sure, I'll try anything to feel better about this," she replied.

"The first thing I do is put in my ear buds and play soft background music on my iPhone. Then I relax in my chair and close my eyes. As I listen to the music, I visualize myself walking through a meadow to my secret garden. I am barefoot, and the grass feels cool beneath my feet.

"The entrance to the garden is a stone archway with a beautiful wooden door. On the outside of the door is a carving of a rose and the word *Namaste*—meaning we are all made from the same One Divine Consciousness.

"As I approach the door, it opens wide, and I walk along a beautiful garden path, shaded by a white trellis covered in lavender wisteria. Along the rock walls of the garden are climbing roses in every color.

"There is a large ivy-covered wall at the far end of the garden and a waterfall cascading over its edge into a small creek.

"Near the waterfall is a daybed suspended by rope from the overhanging branch of a giant oak tree. The bed is covered in flowing white linens and soft pillows. The canopy is draped in white gauze fabric and topped by a set of white, wooden angel wings dipped in gold.

"A gentle breeze is blowing as I climb onto the soft bed and gently swing back and forth. The sun is filtering through the trees, and I can hear the song of the birds and the cascading waterfall.

"I close my eyes, and take a deep, relaxing breath. As I continue taking deep breaths in and out, I imagine a golden ball of light dropping down into my body. This beautiful waterfall of light goes into my mind, calming and relaxing my mind, and washes away any thoughts or energy I do not want. Any resistance just floats away.

"I imagine the light flowing through my heart and clearing away any emotional energy that may be holding me back. I imagine the light filling my body with the energy of serenity, love, abundance, and reassurance. I feel myself floating in this energy.

"In this space of love and serenity, I think of issues I want to resolve and ask my Higher Self, my Soulful Self to give me a higher vision of the issue or to release the issue and take care of it for me.

"I thank my Higher Self, take a nice deep breath in, and slowly open my eyes, knowing that all is well. I gracefully rise from the bed and walk back through the garden, past the waterfall and rose-covered walls, and through the carved wooden gate."

"Wow, I was right there with you," Margie said.

"And how do you feel now?" I asked.

"I feel peaceful and at ease."

"That feeling means you are in vibrational proximity to the answer you are seeking," I said.

"You know what, it's just stuff. It doesn't matter who gets what. They probably don't even care. The only person in pain over this was me. I believed they should have done things differently. But it's done; there's no going back."

"Your power is in your *now*. So now what?"

"I'm still not sure what action to take. If I use this meditation and get to that good feeling place and ask for guidance, how do I know it's the right answer? How do I know I'm not just making it up?"

"You will know by how it feels. That's why it's important to meditate and get into a good feeling place before asking for guidance. The answer is always given. The challenge for most people is that they limit the path of how the answer can reveal itself."

"What do you mean?" she asked.

"For example, you said that you want to know which action to take on dividing up your mom's estate. If you were to receive an answer, how do you expect it would come to you?" I asked.

"Well, it would probably come from my attorney or accountant or maybe even in a dream," Margie said.

"Okay, any other way you can think of?" I asked.

"Not really."

"So, what you have just told the Universe is that you want an answer, and it can only come to you through your attorney or accountant or a dream. When we limit the Universe by our beliefs or expectations of how it will show up, we slow down the process of receiving our desire.

"There are a million ways the Universe can conspire to serve you if you can let go of your attachment to the how."

"You mean all I have to do is feel good, ask for guidance, and allow it to show up?" Margie asked.

"I know it sounds too simple, but that's how it works. The Universe isn't responding to your words, it's responding to how you feel. The more you can feel the essence of your desire and the excitement of receiving it, the faster it manifests. Would you like me to share a funny example that happened to me yesterday?"

"Of course! That would be great," she said.

"I am in the process of writing a book about how our expectations create our reality. And while lying in bed, doing my morning meditation, I asked Source and my guides if I was on the right track. I didn't worry if they would answer, nor was I concerned what the answer would be. I just felt excited about how good it would feel to have clarity. And eager to see how they would surprise and delight me.

"As I got out of bed, my husband walked into our master bathroom. While he was at the bathroom sink, I began making the bed. My cell phone was lying on the nightstand, and when

I walked to the opposite side of the bedroom to pick up some decorative throw pillows, my iPhone dinged and Siri said, 'What can I help you with?'

"I thought, *That's weird*, and before I could reach the phone, Siri said, 'Here's what I found.'

"My husband heard my phone and, standing in the bathroom doorway, asked me what was going on. I told him I didn't know. The phone just went off by itself. I picked up my phone to see what Siri had found, and I started laughing.

"It was a picture of an oil painting titled *Allegory of Hope* by Francesco Guardi, painted in 1747. It depicted a woman carrying a basket of flowers with water behind her and an angel at her feet. Below it was a definition of hope: Hope is an optimistic attitude of mind based on an expectation of positive outcomes related to events and circumstances in one's life or the world at large. As a verb, its definitions include expect with confidence and to cherish a desire with anticipation."

"I looked at my husband and said, 'Hello, Source is calling!'"

"Oh my gosh, Kathy. It was like the vision of you in your secret garden with the water and flowers and angel wings. And the definition talked about expectations like your book. And even the part that said, 'Cherish a desire with anticipation,' it's what you were telling me to do. That was God calling!"

"And isn't it fun? And isn't it crazy? And could I have imagined how Source would answer in a million years?" I asked.

"There's no way you could have planned that," Margie said.

"Just trust that Source always answers, and when you're in a high vibration, feeling good about possibilities, you'll get *the call*."

There are many who fear the unknown. It's important to remember the unknown is full of adventure that will surprise and delight you.

~ Eva Gregory

ᘒᘒᘒ

Something More

God, Source, All That Is knows everything you want, where it is, and your proximity to it. The entire Universe is at work managing the details. But, when you hold beliefs about how things "should" be done and try to control the details, you slow down your manifestation.

When we believe that things "should" happen a certain way, we block all other avenues for receiving our desires. It's like driving to the grocery store the same route every time because it's the route you're familiar with. One day, your route is blocked by road construction, and since you don't trust the alternate route because you've never driven it, you go back home without your groceries.

The Universe is like a giant GPS system that knows every possible route to your desired destination. And even if you make a wrong turn, it can reroute you and get you back on track. The voice of the GPS is your soul, communicating to you on an energetic wavelength that is not detectable by your five senses.

There is no assertion in our attraction-based Universe. Just like there is no assertion in our vehicle's GPS. The GPS won't make us take a new route to make our life easier, it simply offers us guidance. We are free to choose which direction we take.

If you've stayed with me this far, you're beginning to understand that there is much more to this beautiful world than the eyes can see. In fact, most of our world is invisible to the naked eye. Our physical senses pick up only a fraction of what exists in this world.

Just as dogs can hear sounds we cannot and smell scents that we are happy we cannot, there is a vibrational energy field we cannot see. We get a glimpse of it now and then, when a pebble skims across a lake and makes ripples or when the wind blows the leaves on trees.

We experience it at times when the hair on the back of our neck stands up for no apparent reason, or we have an inexplicable knowing when something or someone isn't safe. This internal experience of energy is called intuition, and it cannot be explained in terms of the five senses because it is not a product of the external world. It comes from within.

When I took Margie through my guided meditation, it quieted her "monkey" mind, slowed her breathing, calmed her energy, and within just a minute or two, she felt at peace and her guidance came through. She realized her belief that things "should" be different than they were was the cause of her pain. And she let her story go.

The soul uses intuition to communicate and guide us on our journey. If we want to receive the guidance we are asking for, we must take time to tune into our heart through meditation and mindfulness.

ℰℰℰ

Something for You

Have you ever had the experience of having a sudden insight, an "aha" moment? Did you act on it? Or did you or someone talk you out of it? What was the outcome?

Those moments are guidance from our soul in answer to our asking. By practicing meditation and mindfulness, we strengthen our soul connection and sensitivity to the subtle, quiet voice of intuition. And, over time, we develop trust in our own guidance system above anyone else's opinion.

A few years ago, my husband and I traveled with some friends to the Mediterranean. There were eight of us in the group, including engineers, attorneys, CEOs, and world travelers. On our return trip home, we had to make a connecting flight in Europe. When we disembarked from the jet bridge, it was late and dark outside. Our flight was late arriving to the airport, and we were all rushing to make our connecting flight.

We were unfamiliar with the airport, and all the signs were in a language none of us spoke. So, I asked a security guard who was sitting on a stool, leaning back against the wall, how to get to our connecting airline.

He pointed at two glass doors that led outside and said, "Go through those doors and around."

Monica, a world traveler and strong leader who few people dared to argue with, began to lead the way out the door.

My intuition kicked in, and something told me that this was not the way to our connecting flight. I spoke up and suggested, "Let's go up the stairs and see where that leads before we go outside."

"He just said it's this way. We're going to miss our connecting flight if we don't hurry," Monica replied.

Everyone was tired and frustrated with the situation and agreed with Monica. I said, "Okay," but did not follow them. Instead, I trusted my intuition and went up the stairs. When I opened the door, our airline ticket counter was directly in front of me. I yelled and waved to the others. Luckily, they had paused long enough that they had not been locked out of the terminal.

As everyone rushed up the stairs, the guard leaning back on his stool just shrugged as if it were a big joke.

Monica said, "I'm so sorry I didn't listen to you. How did you know?"

I smiled and said, "My GPS was rerouting me."

Through my daily practice of meditation and mindfulness, I have a deeper connection with my soul and a strong trust of my intuition. That's why I felt confident trusting my inner guidance over the opinions of the CEOs, engineers, attorneys, Monica, and the TSA Agent.

The mind, like Monica, likes to be in charge and voices its opinions as if they are fact. It feels safe when it believes it's in control, and when it doesn't, it reacts out of fear.

So, if you want to create a joy-filled, abundant life, you must integrate your mind, body, breath, and access your intuition. It takes a consistent practice to create strong neural pathways in order trust the quiet inner voice when chaos is all around you.

If you'd like to live as a creator rather than a reactor, if you'd like to live in joy rather than fear, the first step is to create a tool you can use to shift your energy and allow your guidance to come through.

Guided Meditations

- Strengthen your intuition by using guided meditations daily.
- You can either create your own like I did, use the one I shared in this chapter, or use an app like Calm that has hundreds of different types of meditations.
- Set a timer to go off a couple times a day or more.
- Take three to five minutes to calm your mind.
- Once you feel at peace, ask your inner guidance what it would like to tell you, or ask for guidance around a particular topic.
- Breathe and listen.

Sometimes the answer may come instantly; other times it will come later in the day or when you're focused on something else. The more you practice, the more automatically you will begin to listen for the quiet voice of your intuition.

What we choose to call it, God, Source, Guides, Angels, or All That Is, doesn't matter. There is a loving, benevolent life force energy that supports all creation. We sense it when we hear a baby giggle, see a puppy romping through the grass, or hear a dove cooing in the tree. And we can experience it when we are at peace and allow our soul to guide us through our intuition.

There is unlimited support available to you once you tap into your intuition. Siri-ously!

CHAPTER 21

I'm Mom's Favorite

Never the spirit is born.
The spirit will cease to be never.
Never the time when it was not.
End and beginning are dreams,
Birthless and deathless and changeless.
Remaineth the spirit forever.
Death hath not touched it at all!
Dead though the house of it seems.
~ The Bhagavad Ghita, also offered as a Sioux Prayer of Passing

Friday, January 9, 2015

I'm so sorry, Kat. Your mom just passed away."

A heavy sadness enveloped me as I tried to speak. "I was just leaving to visit her. I thought for sure I'd get to say goodbye."

"I know," Shelly said. "I thought she would be with us a while longer too. But, Val, the home care nurse, was with her, so she wasn't alone. She went quietly in her sleep."

I couldn't hold the tears back any longer. I had known she wouldn't be with us much longer, but I guess you're never ready to say goodbye.

"She loved Val," I said, as tears streamed down my face. "They became good friends over the past few months. I'm glad she was there with her."

"Please take your time getting here," Shelly said. "There's no hurry. I've made all the necessary calls to the funeral home, and I called your sisters and brother. I will wait here for you."

When I arrived at Mom's house, her Great Pyrenees, Samson, came bounding up to me. "Samson, what are we going to do with you now, sweetheart?" I asked. As I stroked his chin and thought of what he had meant to Mom, I started crying.

Shelly hugged me and said, "You did such a wonderful job of taking care of your mother. You did everything you could."

"Is Val still here?" I asked.

"She just left a couple of minutes ago. She was pretty upset and didn't want to make things any harder for you and your family."

"Is Mom still here? I saw the hearse out front."

"Yes, when I talked to your brother, he wanted us to wait until he got here before we did anything. And your sister and her family are on their way too."

"I want to say goodbye to Mom. I'll be just a minute," I said.

I don't know what I was expecting, but when I entered the room, I felt as if I was looking at an empty vessel. I reached out and touched her arm to thank her body for doing its best to keep her alive and walked out of the room.

I sat on the couch and started sobbing, realizing that I would never get to hug her again. Samson leaned against me and started licking my tears, which caused me to laugh despite myself.

"He was so gentle with your mom," Shelly said. "He literally tiptoed into her bedroom to see if she was sleeping or awake. If she was sleeping, he would lie next to her bed for hours."

"He's the sweetest, most gentle giant of a dog that I've ever met." I said. "He loves everyone including children, cats, and other dogs. He never growls at anything. He rarely even barks. The first time I heard him bark, it was like a whisper."

"I haven't heard him bark at all, even with all the strangers coming and going," Shelly said. "New nurses show up, and he acts as if he's known them forever. He wags his tail and rolls over to be petted on his tummy."

"He's sweet and extremely smart. One night last year, Mom had been asleep and was awakened by Samson's howling. Mom called to Samson, but he just stayed in the living room howling so loud she thought he was in distress.

"So, Mom got out of bed and went to see what was wrong with him. When she reached down to pet him, she fell to the floor. She was having a heart attack. Mom crawled to the front door and was able to reach up to unlock it, and before she passed out, pulled the phone to the floor and dialed 911.

"Luckily the ambulance was just a block from her house and the EMTs were able to get there in time to resuscitate her. The EMT said if Samson hadn't woken her up, she would have died in her sleep."

"Wow, what an amazing dog."

"He's the perfect dog, except for one little problem," I said.

"What's that?" Shelly asked.

"He has separation anxiety. The people at the animal shelter told us he had been severely abused as a puppy. When their veterinarian found him, she didn't think he would live. It took months for him to recuperate."

"So, what are you going to do with him now?" she asked.

"I'm not sure. I love him and would take him home with me, but we have two large male rescue dogs and two rescue cats. We're already over our homeowner association's two-pet limit."

"Can one of your sisters or your brother take him?"

"They all work, and Samson can't be left alone."

"I could take him for a few days," Shelly offered.

"That is so sweet of you to offer, but he will destroy your house if you leave him alone for more than five minutes. The people at the shelter didn't explain the severity of his anxiety when Mom adopted him.

"For the first two weeks she had him, she took him everywhere and never left him alone. Then, one day, she left him for an hour to go to lunch with a friend. When she got home and pulled in the driveway, he came running up to her from the neighbor's yard across the street.

"When she went inside the house, Samson had trashed every single room. He had pulled furniture out into the middle of the room, ripped open every pillow and cushion. Tore paintings and wall hangings off the wall and chewed them to shreds.

Knocked over tables and chairs. Pulled every set of window blinds and curtains off every window in the house and chewed them beyond recognition.

"He destroyed lamps and rugs and chewed through two sets of wooden room dividers. He dug and chewed through sheet rock on the walls by the door. And since he couldn't scratch through the metal door, he finally jumped through a closed window, cutting himself on the jagged glass.

"Luckily, he healed okay, but it took us days to repair all the damage."

"Wow, it's hard to believe that sweet, mild-mannered Samson would do all that. Especially in just an hour," Shelly said.

"Over time, we were able to train him to stay alone for an hour or two. But, when Mom got sick and had to go into the hospital, he had another episode. So, we started leaving him at a pet resort when she couldn't be home with him.

"Sometimes he was there for a month. He seems to do okay if there are people or other dogs around. But I couldn't guarantee it. I guess I'll have them keep him for now until I can figure out a solution."

Monday, January 12, 2015

The weekend was a whirlwind of planning and making arrangements for Mom's cremation, her celebration of life party, and her burial next to Dad at Ft. Sam Houston Cemetery.

Today, the first three items on my to-do list were to call the animal shelter, call the veterinarian, and check into therapy dog training. I had to find a new home for Samson.

First, I contacted the animal shelter where Mom adopted Samson. They knew Mom was sick and had promised her they would take him back if she couldn't keep him.

"I'm sorry, ma'am, we don't take dogs back once they're adopted," the young receptionist said.

"May I please speak to the director of the shelter?" I asked.

"I'm sorry, ma'am, she's not here at the moment. But, I can tell you she will not take the dog back."

I explained to the receptionist, "The director promised my mom they would find Samson a new home when she agreed to adopt him because he was only a year old, and Mom was having health problems at the time."

"I'm sorry, ma'am, but that director is no longer with the shelter, and we will not honor that agreement."

"Can you look up his records and tell me the name of the veterinarian who treated him?"

"I'm sorry, ma'am. I can't help you. I'm the only one here, and the records are over a year old, and I don't know where they are."

I could feel anger rising in me. I was grieving the passing of my mother and overwhelmed with all the details of handling her affairs, and wanting to find a good home for Samson, and if this young woman said "I'm sorry, ma'am" one more time, I was going to scream.

So, I hung up before I said something I might regret later.

Now, I knew better than to keep pushing to find a solution. I also knew that the receptionist was simply matching my own resistance, and the best thing I could do was find a way to relax and feel better before taking any action.

But, under stress, I defaulted back into my old habits of pushing through and instead made another phone call to the pet resort.

"Hi, Cheryl. This is Kat. Can you do me a favor and look at Samson's dog tags. I think the name of his old vet is still on one of the tags."

"Sure, hold on."

Finally, some cooperation, I thought.

"The tags were pretty faded, Kat, but here's her name. I can't read the phone number though."

"Thanks a bunch. How's Samson doing?"

"Well, he seems a little sad, so he's hanging out with all the employees back in the break room."

"Oh, he's not in a kennel?"

"He's such a great dog that everyone just lets him run around with them during the day. We only put him in a kennel at night. I sure hope you can find him a good home."

"Me too. Thanks so much."

Next, I called the veterinarian's office to see if she would be willing to take him back, or if she knew anyone who could take him in as a foster pet, the way she did when he was injured.

But when I tried to explain the situation, she got angry. "You were supposed to be bringing him to me for his checkups. We keep track of all the dogs we treat, and when I tried to get information from the shelter, I could never get an answer."

Well, at least I'm not the only one who couldn't get any answers, I thought.

"My mom adopted him, and I was with her when she picked him up from the shelter. They never said anything to us, and I didn't even know your name. But my husband has been taking him to our vet, and he's caught up with all his shots."

"Well, we can't take him back, and I don't know anyone who can keep him."

"Can you tell me anything about his anxiety problem?" I asked.

"What anxiety problem? He never had any problems."

At this point, I realized that I needed to shift my vibration before I could find a solution. Things usually went so smoothly for me, and this whole morning had been extremely uncomfortable.

"Okay, thank you for your time," I said. "I'll find him a home."

The path of least resistance = the path of most allowance.
~ Esther and Jerry Hicks-Abraham

I gave up making efforts and decided to go for a walk, eat some lunch, and browse through some decorating magazines. Afterward, I felt much more like my usual calm self and decided to meditate for a few minutes to raise my vibration even more.

In the middle of my meditation I heard: *Ask Mom,* and I started to laugh. It was so obvious, but I had been missing her, so it hadn't occurred to me before.

"Okay, Mom," I said aloud. "Now that you've transitioned and you understand all those discussions we had over the last few months about eternal life, I need your help. Where do you want Samson to go that serves everyone's highest good? Because I can't figure this out."

As soon as I asked the question, I let it go and felt at ease for the first time in several days.

Moments later, my cell phone rang. It was Shelly.

"Hi, Kat. Have you found a home for Samson yet?" she asked.

I smiled to myself and said, "No, as a matter of fact I was just praying and asking Mom what the heck I'm supposed to do with him because neither the shelter nor the vet will take him back."

Shelly laughed and said, "I was just talking to Jennifer, a nurse here at the hospice center, about Samson. Her husband is a disabled veteran who needs a new service dog. His current dog is a Great Pyrenees, like Samson, and needs to be retired in the next year. They are looking for a new dog to train."

"This is Mom's doing for sure," I said. "I had already planned to check into training for him as a therapy dog, but this is even better. My dad was a war veteran, and Mom always tried to help other veterans however she could. Where do they live?"

"Right down the street from you," Shelly said.

"Did you tell Jennifer about Samson's anxiety problem?" I asked.

"Yes, and she said it's not an issue. She's a dog trainer and mentioned that separation anxiety is a typical trait for their breed. And since Samson will be a 24/7 service dog, he'll never be alone anyway."

"I couldn't have planned a better solution if I tried," I said. "Thank you so much, Shelly. I'll give Jennifer a call."

Tuesday, January 13, 2015

"Hi, Jennifer. How did it go at the pet resort?" I asked.

"David loves Samson. He's really excited about having him as his new service dog. In fact, he said even if he didn't qualify for training, he wants to keep him anyway. We plan to bring our other dogs by to meet Samson tomorrow, if that's okay with you."

"Of course. And I'm so happy that you want to keep him no matter what. I know he'll love being around your dogs and kids. Let me know how it goes with the doggie date tomorrow."

"Will do, and thanks again," said Jennifer.

"Oh, I almost forgot. In lieu of flowers for our mom's celebration, my brother and sisters and I have asked our friends and family to donate toward Samson's training."

"I don't know what to say. That's so generous of you all. Are you sure?"

"Positive. We know training can run up to nine or ten thousand dollars. Plus, many of our friends and family are veterans, and it will give them an opportunity to support another vet. Besides, I know for sure it's what Mom would have wanted," I said.

Wednesday, January 14, 2015

"Hey, Sis, I have an idea for Mom's celebration," Diane said. "You know how Mom always liked wearing T-shirts with sayings on them? What if the four of us kids all wear black T-shirts that say, 'I'm Mom's favorite?' And I can get a matching shirt made for Samson that says, 'No, I'm Mom's favorite.'"

"That's hilarious, Diane. It sounds like a prank Mom would pull. She told me that she wanted everyone to remember the good times and to have fun at her celebration. If we can bring in some humor, others will follow suit."

"I'll call and make sure everyone agrees, and then I'll order the shirts," said Diane.

"And I'll call and have Samson groomed and let them know we'll be putting a shirt on him before we go to the celebration."

Saturday, January 18, 2015

A million details had been handled in the past week. It felt like Mom was orchestrating everything, and my job was simply listening to the quiet voice within.

My siblings and I worked together by focusing on our own strengths and allowing each other the freedom to do what we were best at. Our spouses were amazed at how smoothly everything was being handled.

On my way to the celebration, I stopped to pick Samson up from the pet resort. His coat was beautifully groomed, and he allowed me to put the T-shirt on him without a fuss.

"Is that what you're wearing to the funeral?" asked the pet resort manager.

We had decided to keep the gathering casual and comfortable. So, I was wearing blue jeans, my black T-shirt with a stylish lightweight jacket, and cowboy boots.

"Actually, all my siblings are wearing the same T-shirt too," I answered. "And we're not having a funeral. After my dad's somber and sad military burial, Mom decided she didn't want people mourning for her. Instead, she wanted a party to celebrate her life."

"What a great idea. And those T-shirts are a fun way to honor your mom's sense of humor too," she said.

Mom's celebration was being held in the Texas Hill Country on a beautiful piece of property covered in large oak trees. The building was made of Texas limestone with tall ceilings, huge fireplaces, and hardwood floors.

When I arrived, the outdoor patio was being set up with tables and chairs so people could sit inside or outside.

The perfect weather in mid-January was unexpected by most, except me. I had intended a beautiful day, and it was. The sun was shining, a light breeze was blowing, and the temperature was a perfect seventy degrees.

Inside, the food service was being organized by my brother's restaurant, and my brother was hanging poster-sized photos of Mom around the room. My sister-in-law and niece were setting up a video montage of Mom they had created, along with her favorite music so it would play continuously during the event.

My sisters were busy decorating the tables with Mom's favorite fabric, red gingham, and I started filling mason jars with her favorite yellow daises to be used as centerpieces.

As guests started arriving, Samson and I walked outside to greet everyone as they entered.

Our "I'm Mom's Favorite" T-shirts made everyone smile, but the big hit of the celebration was Samson.

"It was such a great idea to raise money to train Samson," my friend Linda said.

"He's a special dog, and he'll be wonderful as a service companion," I said. "And did you know that his name means *second service*? I wonder if Mom knew that when she named him!"

The donation basket quickly began to fill, and people were taking time to introduce themselves to David and Jennifer, who had come to honor Mom.

"Thank you both for coming," I said. "I know you aren't feeling well, David, and I'm so glad you could make it. Meeting you personally has made a big difference in the amount of donations being collected."

"I'm just so glad that Samson gets along great with our dogs," David said. "When we brought our dogs to meet him in the common area at the kennel, they ran and played as if they'd always been together."

"When do you think you'll be taking him home?" I asked.

"In about another week," Jennifer said.

Tears welled up in my eyes at the thought of saying goodbye to Samson. So, I excused myself and took Samson for a walk in the field at front of the property, away from the crowd.

We walked around for a while, enjoying the beautiful day. When I sat on the grass, he lay beside me and put his head in my lap.

"It's been a long year for both of us, hasn't it, Samson," I said as I stroked his head. "You kept Mom's spirits up and gave her a reason to live. I will always love you for that, sweet boy. You really were Mom's favorite."

How lucky I am to have known somebody and something that saying goodbye to is so damned awful.
~ Evans G. Valens, *The Other Side of the Mountain*

Something More

We always have free will. We can choose to focus on the sorrow of goodbyes or on the joy of a life well lived, on failure or success, fear or love. In this world of polarities, we will experience it all, yet our happiness depends on deliberately reaching for the thought that feels better.

The Universal Law of Polarity is the principle that everything has two poles or opposites. For example, hot water is the opposite of cold water. Even though these opposites may appear to be two separate things, they're actually two inseparable parts of the same thing. They are both water at different temperature extremes.

And within the polarities of hot and cold, perceptions vary depending on the perceiver. Have you ever stepped into a shower where someone else had preset the water control to their perfect temperature and been shocked by a blast of cold water? What's considered hot or cold will vary from one person to another with lots of variables in between. We get to have them all.

We each have unique dreams and desires. That's why it's important to focus on what you want and to allow others to have what they are having. You wouldn't continue standing in a cold shower, cursing the cold. It doesn't change anything. You'd simply turn the water knob to your desired temperature.

Likewise, when you have thoughts or situations that don't feel good, don't keep standing in the shower of the unwanted; simply turn your focus to what you do want.

The Law of Polarity exists so we have an unlimited buffet of choices to choose from. Imagine a buffet with every food you love, every food you dislike, and all the foods you have yet to try. I love pizza, but you'd never catch me eating oysters. My friend loves oysters but doesn't eat gluten. Is one choice wrong or right, good or bad? All buffet items are simply available to us, and we get to choose. And the way we choose is by our attention and our vibration.

As Abraham-Hicks likes to say, there are two ends to every stick. The end of the stick that has what you want on it and the opposite end of the stick that has what you don't want. If you don't want oysters, don't put them on your plate by spending your time, focus, and energy on telling others how much you hate oysters. Just enjoy your pizza.

What's important to understand is each situation in life, regardless of how you may currently perceive it, has within it the possibility to experience the opposite. Everything has a built-in duality.

Up and down, black and white, sickness and health, birth and death. You can't have one side of a continuum without the other. If we didn't have darkness, how would we know light? If we didn't have sadness, how would we know joy?

ᘓᘓᘓ

Something for You

The results we see in our lives, whether wanted or unwanted, are determined by how we choose to perceive something. When I called the animal shelter and kept meeting resistance, which grew with every "I'm sorry, ma'am," I hung up the phone because I knew I needed to choose a different perspective before moving ahead.

But, because I was grieving the loss of my mom, I defaulted back into pushing forward without taking time to meditate and shift my energy. So, I met up with the same resistance when I contacted the veterinarian. Is resistance a "bad" thing? How would we know what we want if we never bumped up against what we don't want? Resistance is just one way the Universe reminds us to let go of judgments, focus on our desires, and allow miracles into our lives.

Once I took the time to center myself through self-care and meditation, my inner guidance showed me I was carrying a story, a perspective, a judgment that the rejection by the shelter and the veterinarian was a "bad" thing.

Within every perceived problem there is a solution. Knowing that the Law of Polarity is a continuum that allows for "bad" to become "good," I became curious. "What if there's a better solution, and this perceived rejection is leading me to the answer I'm seeking?"

By being curious, I shifted my perception, which raised my vibration, and the answer unfolded with ease and grace through Shelly. I didn't have to figure anything out. I simply trusted that God/Source would provide a solution and surrendered my need to know how.

Samson needed constant companionship to remain calm. His anxiety problem had within it the seed of the solution. Who would benefit from an animal companion 24/7? A war veteran with chronic pain and PTSD who needed constant companionship. They were a vibrational match.

The Law of Polarity is neutral. It contains the full continuum, and each of us gets to choose our perspective of what is good for us. When we put our attention on any subject, we automatically activate both ends of the stick, wanted and unwanted. That's why it's important to pay attention to which end of the stick you're giving your attention to. Your emotional guidance system will always let you know by the way you feel.

Samson loved to play fetch, so I thought it only fitting to create an acronym in his honor to remind us that life is supposed to be fun.

Play FETCH

F – **Focus** on what you want. Look for the good in everyone and everything.

E – **Expect** things to work out for you even when they don't go as you planned.

T – **Trust** your intuition and trust that God/Source/All That Is has your back and knows the path of least resistance to your desires.

C – **Curiosity** opens your life to miracles. Be curious about new possibilities.

H – **Happiness** happens when we integrate body, mind, and Spirit (breath) in the service of love. Love yourself, and the world will reflect that love back to you.

Living a joyful life requires that we honor the full continuum by experiencing both ends of the spectrum: grief, worry, and frustration as well as joy, bliss, and love. How you choose to focus determines how you experience life.

He who lives in harmony with himself lives in harmony with the Universe.

~ Marcus Aurelius

Conclusion

Love the life you came to live.
Live the best you have to give.

~ Kat Wells

If you've read this far and implemented some of the tools and practices at the end of each chapter, you have a heart of courage. It takes courage to look at what you've unconsciously created in your life that no longer serves you.

It takes courage to take responsibility for your happiness and be a conscious creator. Wherever you are on your journey is perfect. You are right on track for an abundant and exciting life.

When I began writing this book, I had no idea it would start with my father's funeral and end with my mother's. Nor that the new edition would be inspired by the loss of my husband and a world-wide pandemic. And yet, there is a gift in that for me. Blessed awareness of how far I have come on my journey back to joy, and the realization that happiness is a choice.

The contrast of my experience at my father's funeral—where I was full of anger, blame, and resentment—to that of my mother's—where I experienced love, compassion, and appreciation—is evidence to me that my happiness was always about my perception and beliefs.

Yet, even with this awareness, the grief I experienced with my husband's death was so devastating, I didn't know if I would survive it this time. In the moment I became a widow, the life I lived and loved for thirty years simply disappeared.

I found myself on a bridge between two worlds. On one end was my old life, and on the other was a new life I couldn't yet imagine.

Although it took almost three years for me to cross the bridge, it was a necessary part of my journey back to wholeness. It showed me that I was supported in my life, and I began to trust again, hope again, laugh and smile again.

The void left by loss was fertile ground to bring in something more beautiful than what was left behind. I have experienced greater happiness, connection, excitement, and love than ever before.

Understanding the Universal Laws and creating a life you love doesn't mean you will never feel sorrow or have a bad day. In this world of polarity, we must have the contrast to experience joy and happiness.

Yet, when you understand that you are the creator of your life, you get to choose how you experience every moment. And, your emotional guidance system lets you know what you are creating. The name of the emotion doesn't matter. If it feels good, you are creating toward your desires; if it feels bad, you are not.

It's not a personal issue of your worthiness, your value, or integrity. It's simply about how many times you have thought that thought. If the thought feels bad, change the thought, which changes your vibration, which changes your life.

You are Magnificence. You are Love. You are the Hero you've been looking for. Everything you need to live an abundant, happy life is within you, now.

Be easy about all of this. There is no finish line because there's always something more— more to love, more to learn, more to live.

Acknowledgments

I am deeply thankful to my beloved Regents Professor of English, Robb Jackson, for acknowledging my gift for writing so that I could believe in myself. I miss you and know that you are guiding me from the other side of the Veil.

I am grateful to Sam Horn for her support and guidance in helping me discover my voice. Thank you, Sam, for your encouragement and sense of humor when I needed it most.

To Keith and Maura Leon, thank you for your patience, love, creativity, and support for the first edition of this book. Not only are you amazing at what you do, but you were there for me when my mother and best friend passed away, and I am forever grateful.

To Esther and Jerry Hicks, and Abraham (the Guide), I am in deep appreciation for your wisdom and guidance. When I met you, my life changed dramatically. I finally understood my true magnificence and how to create the beautiful life I always wanted. It is because of you this book exists.

Thanks to my mentors and spiritual teachers: Eva Gregory, Christy Whitman, Evelyn Apostolou, Karen Wilson, Dr. Sue Morter, Debbie Johnson, Denise Mange, and Julie Kleinhans. You are my angels. There are no words to express the gratitude I feel for you all. Your love, wisdom, and guidance have allowed me to soar. You are the wind beneath my wings.

To my best friends and travel buddies, Richard and Rebecca Durham, thank you for your love and for all the fun adventures we have shared together. It has meant more to me than you will ever know. And thanks to my dear Rebecca: I feel you with me, but I have to say I still haven't quite gotten over you leaving this world so soon. I love you both to the moon and back.

Thanks to my mother and father for agreeing to share this journey with me and for being my first teachers. I love you and feel your love for me. Every time I hear the song "Moonlight Serenade," I can see you dancing among the stars.

To my brother and sisters—thank you for being there for me through the years. It has been a wild and crazy ride, and I love and appreciate you all.

To my beloved, late husband, Mark. Thank you for loving me the way that you did, for always believing in me and supporting my dreams, even when I was ready to give up. You are forever in my heart.

And a special heartfelt thank you to my new publisher and friend, Christine Kloser, for all your guidance, support, and patience as the new edition of this book unfolded. To Carrie Jareed, Jean Merrill, my editor Jennifer Crosswhite, and the Capucia Publishing team, your expertise and support made this book possible, and I am forever grateful.

I am especially grateful for the new love in my life, Greg Davis. Our love is of the Divine, orchestrated one miracle at a time. Thank you for helping me to create a life more beautiful than the one I left behind.

Next Steps

To learn more about coaching with Kat, meet her at
KatWellsInternational.com
and
TheresGotToBeSomethingMore.com

About the Author

Bestselling author, Law of Attraction expert, and mindset mentor, Kat Wells has known hardship. From experiencing abuse, bankruptcy, divorce, and miscarriage to losing her job, her home, her health, and wanting to end her life, Kat realized there had to be *something more* to life.

By immersing herself in the studies of energy and spirituality for more than two decades, she transformed her life, manifesting a marriage of twenty-eight years, financial freedom, two beautiful homes, traveling the world for eight years, vibrant health, and a career she loves.

Kat graduated summa cum laude from Texas A&M University and trained under Dr. Sue Morter, founder of Morter Institute for BioEnergetics. She is a certified Energy Codes Master Trainer and founder of Kat Wells International.

Kat provides coaching, seminars, and workshops using her uncommon blend of experiences and her knowledge of energy, psychology, and the Universal Laws to empower individuals and organizations to realize their full potential.

She spends her time coaching, writing, traveling, and cruising around the Texas Hill Country in her little yellow Jeep.

www.ingramcontent.com/pod-product-compliance
Lightning Source LLC
Chambersburg PA
CBHW051004140626
46546CB00016B/271